It's Not Me,
It's You

It's Not Me, It's You

Subjective Recollections from a
Terminally Optimistic, Chronically Sarcastic,
and Occasionally Inebriated Woman

STEFANIE WILDER-TAYLOR

Simon Spotlight Entertainment
New York   London   Toronto   Sydney

SIMON SPOTLIGHT ENTERTAINMENT
A Division of Simon & Schuster, Inc.
1230 Avenue of the Americas
New York, NY 10020

Certain names and identifying characteristics have been changed and some events compressed, reordered, and expanded.

First Simon Spotlight Entertainment hardcover edition July 2009

SIMON SPOTLIGHT ENTERTAINMENT and colophon are trademarks of Simon & Schuster, Inc.

For information about special discounts for bulk purchases, please contact Simon & Schuster Special Sales at 1-866-506-1949 or business@simonandschuster.com.

The Simon & Schuster Speakers Bureau can bring authors to your live event. For more information or to book an event contact the Simon & Schuster Speakers Bureau at 1-866-248-3049 or visit our website at www.simonspeakers.com.

Designed by Kyoko Watanabe

Manufactured in the United States of America

1   3   5   7   9   10   8   6   4   2

Library of Congress Cataloging-in-Publication Data
Wilder-Taylor, Stefanie.
It's not me, it's you : subjective recollections from a terminally optimistic, chronically sarcastic, and occasionally inebriated woman / by Stefanie Wilder-Taylor
p. cm
Included bibliographical references and index.
ISBN 978-1-4169-5414-9 (alk. paper)
ISBN 978-1-4391-6432-7 (ebook)
1. Wilder-Taylor, Stefanie. 2. Wilder-Taylor, Stefanie—Family.
3. Women—United States—Biography. 4. Women comedians—
United States—Biography. 5. Television writers—United States—Biography.
6. Los Angeles (Calif.)—Biography. 7. Wilder-Taylor, Stefanie—Humor.
8. Interpersonal relations—Humor. 9. American with and humor. I. Title.
CT275.W558614A3 2009
920.72—dc22
[B]
2009004750

For Jon, obviously.

Contents

It's Not Me,
It's You

Nam Myo Ho Renge Kyo

I'll admit it. I can *on occasion* be a bit of a sucker: I once accidentally owned an aggressive dog that was half pit bull because he just looked so darn sweet at the pound. I also once or *twice* spent more than a hundred dollars on an antiwrinkle cream because the salesgirl looked so horrified by my "laugh lines," and I did take fen-phen for about three months when it was all the rage but I stopped not *too* long after I found out it could cause irreparable damage to my heart valves. But I'm definitely not a sucker across the board: I do not find Lance Armstrong inspirational—yes, I know he won the Tour de France like a hundred times with only one ball, but he also divorced his wife who stood by him through the cancer ordeal, broke up with Sheryl Crow, and seems to have topped off his douchery by allegedly screwing an Olsen twin. So no, Lance, you're not fooling me no matter how many damned bracelets you've sold. I've also never joined a pyramid scheme, bought anything from a TV infomercial with the word "miracle" in its name, or truly believed I'd come home ahead from a trip to Vegas. So it may come as a surprise that I once came a little too close for comfort to joining a cult.

I've never been approached by so many "culty" people than when I first moved to Los Angeles. It's almost like cult members can sniff out a recent arrival's feelings of displacement, need for direction, and lack of housing like those drug-sniffing dogs at the airport. I'd already fended off offers from Lifespring and the Forum for weekend "seminars" to improve my life. I'd turned down a "free personality test," the results of which would definitely tell me that I have a strong need to join the Church of Scientology. And then there was the time I deflected a Hare Krishna who tried to startle me into shaving my head, selling flowers, and living on lentil soup by popping out from behind a bush to talk to me about the healing grace of Krishna. I might have even stopped to chat, but, unlike Natalie Portman or Sinead O'Connor, bald is not a hairstyle that's at all flattering on me.

On this particular day, my defenses were down. I'd arrived in Los Angeles from Massachusetts a week prior with my friend Beth Moskowitz. Our original plan was to stay with one of my childhood friends, Tanya, at her aunt's apartment in Hollywood. Tanya made it sound like we were totally set up with a place to stay for at least a week or two while we looked for our own pad. What Tanya failed to mention was that she was flat broke, unemployed, a hot mess, and not getting along with her aunt, who wanted her out as soon as possible. Tanya's aunt begrudgingly let us stay there since her niece had promised, but she didn't trust Tanya, who'd been freeloading off of her for months. Apparently, Tanya had been making long-distance phone calls and not paying the bill, so her aunt had taken to unplugging the phone and bringing it to work with her during the day. We were desperately trying to find an apartment of our own but had to make all of our classified section inquiry calls from a pay phone in front of the nearby Mayfair Market and then stand around waiting for apartment managers to call back. We had thought of buying a cheap phone and hooking it up while her aunt was at work, but Tanya's aunt was one step ahead of us and locked us all out of the apartment during the day.

So we set up a makeshift headquarters in front of the bay of pay phones, making calls from one and waiting for call-backs from the other one, which entailed a strict enforcement of not letting anyone else use the phone. If a random passerby tried to pick up the receiver, we'd intercept immediately: "Is it an emergency?" one of us would ask, placing a palm over the coin slot. One man approached the phone quickly. He had a Dalmatian with him on a leash and he made a lunge for the receiver. "Whoa, whoa, whoa. Sorry, sir, we're using this one."

"But you're not on it."

"We're waiting for an important call."

"Yeah, well I need to call my wife and tell her I found our dog. I've been searching for Bingo for two hours and my wife's worried sick," the guy said as he made another attempt to reach for the phone. But we stood firm.

"I understand your dilemma, but if we let you use the phone it sets a precedent. Then we'd have to let everyone use it. And then where would we be? Not in a two-bedroom apartment with wall-to-wall carpeting, a stove, and refrigerator. That's for sure," I explained, rationally. Bingo's owner gave us a nasty look and shook his head but dragged his dog farther down the block to the corner deli.

Now, since Tanya's aunt's house was not working out, the situation was quite dire. Between the three of us, we weren't the best credit risk. Unfortunately, we hadn't thought of that. Just like it hadn't occurred to us that when you live on your own you have to buy things like sponges and toilet paper. I somehow thought these items just appeared in the cabinets. Sure, I'd seen them in stores, but I had very few recollections of cash transactions taking place.

This particular morning it was above a hundred degrees in the shade and we were all awaiting death by sunstroke when two well-dressed ladies in their forties or fifties approached us. The more outgoing of the two stepped forward and introduced herself as Marcie Walters. Then, nice as can be, Marcie asked if we'd like to join them at a meeting that was being held right around the corner. I was immediately suspicious. I'd seen enough horror movies to know that you just don't trust superfriendly strangers; they are scary and probably want something from you. Like your unborn baby. On the other hand, the other woman was Asian and in my experience it's rare to find an Asian woman who's up to no good.

"What kind of *meeting*?" I asked, carefully emphasizing the word "meeting" for all I was worth to show that I'm not gullible. "It's not AA, is it?" I wasn't going to fall for that again.

"No, no, nothing like that. We belong to a group called Soka Gakkai International. We're Buddhists."

"Buddhists? Are you the ones who can't drink coffee?" Tanya interjected.

"No, that's Mormons." Still, it didn't sound good. I looked at my friends, who were staring at me like I was engaging in small talk with the Menendez brothers, so I turned back to the women.

"Sorry . . . I don't think so," I said sternly.

"There's air-conditioning."

Five minutes later, Tanya, Beth, and I found ourselves in the back of a climate-controlled living room seated on giant Oriental floor pillows, sipping Crystal Light lemonade and watching various people chant "Nam Myo Ho Renge Kyo" over and over in front of a big shrine that had an apple in it. Every so often someone would ring a bell.

Marcie sat next to me and explained what we were seeing—apparently in code. "The workings of the universe are an expression of a single principle, which is the essence of the Lotus Sutra. By putting our lives in rhythm with this law, we can unlock our hidden potential—and achieve creative harmony with the environment." I had no clue what she was talking about, but I nodded my head like I was simply taking in a recipe for BBQ chicken.

"Mmmhmm." I wondered if there was any sort of stronger refreshment option.

"We say the words while thinking of things we want. We can actually manifest these things into our lives just by repeating our mantra 'Nam Myo Ho Renge Kyo.'"

"You mean, like chanting for world peace or ending hunger in Third World countries?" I asked, pretty sure I knew where she was going with this New Agey business.

"No. Like a Gucci bag or a career in radio broadcasting."

"Interesting."

This actually made more sense, because her acrylic manicure with one gold pinky nail wasn't really throwing off a spiritual vibe. Chanting for material things sounded wrong somehow, kind of antispiritual—who knew if I'd only repackaged the idea and called it *The Secret* I could be living in a solid-gold castle, with four entire rooms dedicated just to hats, eating caviar by the fistful and enjoying newly released movies in my giant screening room every night.

"Why don't you give it a try?" Marcie nudged. At this point, Tanya and Beth had fled to the kitchen, where I have no doubt they were rummaging for cookies. But I felt it would be rude not to at least try to get into the spirit of the thing since I was in no great hurry to get back outside. I took a seat on the floor and chanted along with the rest of the group. I felt a little self-conscious, but everyone else was doing it. *Please let me find a new apartment,* I thought over and over in my head. Since Tanya and Beth refused to have anything to do with this, it was obvious I would have to do all the heavy lifting. What was wrong with them? Did they think a new apartment was just going to magically appear? No, you have to work for things in life—which is exactly what I was doing.

When the meeting broke up, a few members, led by Marcie, surrounded us to ask for our information and see how we liked the meeting and to invite us to chant with them again. For some reason, I dutifully gave them Tanya's aunt's address and phone number just to get them off our backs but told them that although we enjoyed ourselves and appreciated their hospitality, we were in a period of transition and would just like to go ahead and chant on our own.

"Well, you're going to need a gohonzon, which is the sacred scroll, and you'll need a cabinet to build your shrine and a bell and special incense," a guy named Atlas said way too intensely. "You can't just use any old incense." Since there was no mention of the shrine's apple, I supposed it was okay to get one at the grocery store, but I had a sneaking suspicion it would need a special forty-dollar blessing at the very least. Then they told us about a meeting that was happening that very Sunday at their corporate headquarters, where we could get all the supplies we needed to be part of the SGI organization.

"No, thanks," I said, shifting my weight back and forth.

I had to pee like crazy, but I was starting to have a creepy feeling they weren't going to let us leave.

"You have to come to the meeting. We won't take no for an answer," Atlas said.

"Okay," Tanya replied. "We'll think about it. But we have to run."

Atlas followed us out. "I'd really like to talk to you more about Soka Gakkai International and what it can bring into your life . . ." We broke into a run.

"What the fuck was that about?" Beth wanted to know on our way back to the Mayfair Market. "I can't believe you were chanting. Those people were batshit crazy!"

Three days later, it was the weekend and we were hanging out at Tanya's aunt's house, enduring her glares, when the phone rang—a sound we rarely got to hear during the week so it was a bit startling. Tanya's aunt answered it. "It's for you guys. It's the intercom. There are some people here to take you to a meeting?"

"Oh my God, they're *here*? This is insane. We'd never agreed to go to the meeting," Beth said, panicking.

"Just ignore them," Tanya's aunt said sensibly, although she was probably secretly disappointed that we wouldn't be leaving the house for the afternoon and more likely helping ourselves to her sandwich supplies.

"Yeah, no shit. We're not *going*," Tanya added. "Hang up the phone!"

It immediately rang again.

And again. And again. And again. Like out of a horror

movie. I almost expected someone to scream, "Oh my God! It's coming from inside the house!" Finally, I picked up the receiver. "We're not going to the meeting so please leave, okay?" and with that I hung up. We nervously peeked out the window of the apartment building. From our vantage on the twelfth floor, we had a clear view of the driveway. There, pulled up to the phone used to call up to the tenants' residences was a carload of people. A couple of them had gotten out and were walking toward the building—of course, Atlas was in the mix.

"Holy shit, they're going to try and get in!" I yelled. We all stayed quiet, praying that no one was going to randomly open the front security door for a couple of seemingly well-dressed psychotics. I think at this exact point in my life I became completely jaded. *Man,* I thought, *if you can't wander into someone's living room and chant for a while without being afraid of repercussions, what* can *you do?*

Twenty seconds later there was pounding on the door. We stayed stock-still and waited for the terror to end. But it didn't. The Buddhist zombies were now yelling outside the door about how we promised and that we should at least come out and talk with them. Finally, I yelled, "We are calling the police if you don't leave right now! I mean it. The phone is in my hand."

It got quiet. And then, slowly, we heard footsteps retreating from the doorway.

"I swear to God you need to find another place to go or I am changing the locks tomorrow," Tanya's aunt said.

The next day was Monday and from our spot at the Mayfair Market, we got the news that we'd been approved for an apartment *with a stove and refrigerator* and it was ready for us to move in. It was a huge stroke of luck—or was it? Just in case, I chanted, "Nam Myo Ho Renge Kyo" all the way back to Tanya's aunt's.

Hollywood Square

My first car was a banana yellow Mazda GLC. Clearly it was not my first choice. It had already logged about 95,000 miles when I snagged it for the low, low price of one thousand dollars, which I financed at over twenty percent interest since I had worse credit than most homeless people. *"But hey, I'd have this bad boy all paid off within three years!"* I thought smugly. I acquired the car out of necessity when I lost all family car privileges.

Close to the day I turned seventeen, having obtained a learner's permit months before and *almost* mastering the three-point turn, I took the road test and much to everyone's surprise, most especially my own, got my driver's license. Three months later, I promptly totaled my parents' thirdhand gold Toyota Corolla—although I'm thinking the good people at Toyota called it gold because it sounded more palatable than bile, which would actually be a more accurate description of the color. So, in retrospect, I probably did them a favor. And not just because of the color but because the car had seen better days—most of which were before I was born. In fact, most of my parents' used cars had the life span of a goldfish. One day the car would be making a strange rattling noise and the next day it would be tires up, only to be replaced by another one just like it with even more miles. Many of my most vivid childhood memories are of being stranded on the side of the road due to a broken water pump, leaky engine gasket, or some other terminal car malady, enduring pitying looks from people driving by in cars manufactured in a more recent decade.

There were four of us girls in the car the night of the crash, coming home from a keg party, singing loudly along to Grandmaster Flash's "White Lines," when I pulled out of an intersection and out of nowhere—or at least out of the direction I wasn't looking—a van smashed into us. The Corolla spun around a few times and came to rest on top of a median. The van kept right on going. Obviously the driver had been drinking even more than we had and had no inter-est in sticking around and coming face-to-face with anyone in possession of a Breathalyzer test. I kind of understood, but maybe a quick, "Yo, anyone dead back there?" or "Sorry to hit and run!" would've taken the sting out a little.

Sitting on the curb with my friends who were all un-scathed but shaken, I contemplated the real harm that would come to me when my parents found out.

As soon as I was dropped off at home by my friend Beth's

parents sans Corolla (which had to be towed to the nearest junkyard), I told my parents what happened. Shockingly, they reacted like they were in some kind of black-and-white sitcom where the parents were polite and slept in separate twin beds.

"Oh, honey, thank goodness you're okay!" my mom said, throwing her arms around me in a startlingly uncharacteristic manner. I was momentarily taken aback.

"But, the car—it's . . . it's totaled," I sobbed, waiting for a weighty object to be hurled in my direction. My mother had been known to throw things in anger and unfortunately she was in the midst of a "pressure-canning her own preserves" phase so she had ready access to those heavy glass jars— which, trust me, are pretty scary coming at you like a fastball pitch from across the room.

At the very *least* I imagined I would get a lecture on how irresponsible I was, how they knew this would happen, how I would have to pay them back for the damage. How none of this would've happened if I'd gotten my goddamn bangs cut so they wouldn't be hanging in my eyes.

"As long as no one was hurt. Cars can be replaced; people can't." *Yeah, sure, Mom.* I'd seen *Invasion of the Body Snatchers.* This pod person wasn't fooling me. I braced myself for the punishment I knew would come. It took a week.

Following a fairly minor infraction, where I missed my curfew by about five minutes, my mother flew into a rage. "If you're not responsible enough to get home at the time I've des- ignated for you, then you are not responsible enough to drive the family car—ever again." To the outside eye, this would seem like an overreaction—I'd seen it coming a mile away.

"How am I going to get around? Go to work?"

"I guess you'll have to buy your own car."

Enter the only car I could afford: the banana yellow Mazda.

A year later, I slapped a "gas, grass, or ass: no one rides for free" sticker on its bumper and took off to make a new life for myself in Los Angeles. I could smell the freedom of the open road—I could also *see* it due to a gaping hole in the driver's side floor of the car, where it had rusted clean through. The GLC's health was declining quickly. Besides the rust holes, the engine sounded louder than a leaf blower; it puffed out huge clouds of white smoke when it started up, and the poor thing could only go 45 mph on the freeway, much to the aggravation of other drivers. Although I don't see why they needed to honk and give me the finger. Did they think I *wanted* to drive that slowly in the fast lane?

By the time I got settled in my new home and realized the mandatory amount of driving a person does in a place like LA, I started to worry. The cross-country trip had taken its toll and the GLC was on its last spark plug. I couldn't even take it on the freeway anymore, seeing as it wouldn't go fast enough to merge and in LA people didn't just give you the finger, they pulled out heavy artillery. I needed a new car desperately.

The little transportation available wasn't an option. I certainly wouldn't be caught dead taking the bus. That was for poor people—not women like me who had over two hundred dollars between her checking and savings accounts. But, by this point, I had even worse credit than ever. I hadn't paid a bill since I'd moved, including a credit card my mom had cosigned for me, which I quickly ran up to the tune of two grand. Turns out these credit card companies don't care what your financial situation is; they want a payment *every* month, and I was under a constant barrage of calls from collection agencies. Because caller ID had yet to be invented, I was often forced to pick up the phone and say hello, only to hear a telltale pause and then an unfamiliar voice mispronounce my name.

"May I please speak to Stefanie Willer?" That would be my cue to fake my voice like I was suddenly an elderly Hispanic woman.

"Uh . . . *hola?*" I'd say, trying to sound like I'd also just been roused from a sound sleep at two in the afternoon to add to the confusion.

"I'm looking for Stefanie Widler? Wil-dair?"

"Ooo . . . *no habla ingles.*"

That would usually hold them off for a good hour. But then they'd call again. I wondered if this approach from bill collectors actually worked on anyone. Did they think they could simply annoy you into making a payment? If I didn't have money on Tuesday afternoon, there was a *very* strong possibility I wouldn't be rolling in piles of hundreds by Wednesday morning. Also, the mere fact that I'm *home* on a Tuesday afternoon should be a tip-off that I'm *not working*— and therefore have no money.

As a last resort, I called my mother to see if there was a slim chance she could help me out. I knew she wouldn't cosign a car loan seeing as how she was still a bit miffed about the "credit card incident," which she'd ended up paying off so I didn't ruin her credit as well. I had to ask for the money straight-out. I explained how bad I needed a car so that I could get to work to earn money for necessities, like groceries, and possibly a few luxuries, like going to the dentist. Otherwise, I'd be forced to do something drastic, like . . . go to college.

She told me that she'd think about it.

A week later, she came up with the following plan: I would work and save up a decent amount of money, a few thousand dollars maybe, and she would match whatever funds I raised so that I could buy myself a car, which would seem like a very sensible solution—provided I wasn't looking to purchase a car in *this century.* I couldn't understand her logic. Did she think I was moonlighting as Donald Trump? I was working a part-time minimum-wage job, barely surviving on Top Ramen and bologna sandwiches. By the time I had saved up enough money to buy *half* a car, I wouldn't need one because our society would most likely be using jet packs to buzz around the sky as their sole means of personal transportation. I needed a car *now.* I tried to reiterate this to my mother, but all I remember from her response was "blah blah, time to learn responsibility, blah blah, cars aren't free . . . blah." Obviously, this plan was not going to work.

My mother had to be wrong. Hell, I lived in Los

Angeles—land of opportunity! And that's when it hit me. It was so obvious it may as well have been tattooed on my face: Go on a game show. It was so brilliant, I almost laughed out loud. Why hadn't I thought of this sooner? From my youngest days I've had a borderline obsessive love of game shows. It was just a matter of picking which one. This was a stressful decision. It was one thing to lie on my couch eating dry salami and saltines, screaming "dumbass" at the lady in the Christmas tree sweater vest on *The Price Is Right* who couldn't decide if two bars of Dove soap cost more than a box of Rice-A-Roni, but quite another to be on national television doing it yourself. Whatever show I chose would have to be easy. *Wheel of Fortune* was definitely out. As much as I liked watching the show, I was usually the very last person on the planet to figure out the puzzle. The board could literally be missing the A from "Jack and Jill" and I'd be completely stumped. Surely I would've eaten up any winnings I made from solving the puzzle just buying vowels alone. Had to rule out *Family Feud;* could not risk the off-chance they might randomly drug test, a huge red flag for key team members.

After a few more days of research done from the comfort of my bed, I hit upon a perfect show: *Hollywood Squares*. It fit all my criteria. Big prizes? Check. Almost indiscernible skill level required? Check. Basic understanding of tic-tac-toe strategy? Uh, check. From the looks of things, all I had to do was agree or disagree with the celebrities' answers to random questions; the possible looking like an asshole factor was up to them. New car, here I come!

Seated on bleachers in an ice-cold studio with about sixty other *Squares* hopefuls, I felt slightly less confident. We were supposed to stand, say our name, and tell one interesting fact about ourselves. From the way everyone was overly enthusiastically whooping it up, being a game show contestant required a lot of undignified clapping and jumping up and down as well as a lack of sanity. One guy with psycho eyes, a huge mustache, and cowboy attire popped up out of turn and yelled so loudly you would've thought the entire group of us was hearing impaired.

"My name's Robert, but my friends call me Crazy Red. I collect Barbie dolls and I'm a proud poppa to ten children! I just know I'm perfect for your show!" In my mind, the only thing Crazy Red seemed perfect for was a vasectomy—but the casting director was practically salivating. I didn't feel good about my chances. The only thing I could think of to say about myself was that I had an unnatural love affair with chimps and I'd always wanted to keep one as a pet. So no one was more shocked than I was when the call came in a week later that I was picked for the show.

That's how I found myself in a holding room backstage with a handful of other chosen people waiting for a competing contestant to be knocked out or win a car, giving one of us a chance to get out there. In the meantime, we were being run through tic-tac-toe strategy drills like new recruits in game show boot camp.

"Lisa, if George goes to the left upper corner with his X, and the middle is already taken, what should be your next move?" barked Tom, the nineteen-year-old tyrant in charge of our group, which, naturally, included Big Red.

"Um, I'll take Jim J. Bullock?" Lisa said, growing unsure of herself. It was understandable. We'd been coming to the studio all day for three days straight waiting for our chance to get on the show. Three eight-hour days with nothing to eat but old triangles of American cheese sandwiches, lukewarm honeydew melon slices, and a pot of burnt Folgers coffee was starting to take its toll.

"You can't just say, 'I'll take Jim J. Bullock.' You need to say, 'I'll take Jim J. Bullock to *block*!'" Duh.

"Okay, you're gonna need to bring your energy *way* up!" Tom scolded us. I bet this type of pep talk worked like a charm in the bedroom. Personally, I thought my energy *was* way up, considering I normally have less energy than a houseplant. I felt I should be given props for even attempting to feign interest in a roomful of future scrapbookers. The whole situation was getting irritating to me because I didn't need their boot camp. I was ready for battle. While these yahoos had been home beefing up their tic-tac-toe game, I'd been watching the show every night preparing for Operation Win a New Car. Like a spy studying the enemy, I'd learned that Joan Rivers, the center square at the time, was always right. It wasn't clear if the producers slipped her the correct answers or if she was just some sort of game show savant, and it really didn't matter—disagree with Joan at your own peril. The rest was even simpler: With any multiple choice question, the least obvious answer was always right; true/false questions, no matter how ridiculous they sounded, were always true. "True or false: In Virginia it's illegal to take a nap with a camel?" Absolutely true. I have no idea why the writers at the time never mixed it up more, but I thank them for it.

When it was finally my turn at the podium, I was ready. Too bad I hadn't put as much thought into my style choice. True, it was the eighties, but it would have been helpful if someone had sent me a letter from the future warning me that wearing huge shoulder pads would prove to be a regrettable idea. So since I will never let anyone watch the VHS tape of the show, people just have to trust me when I tell them that I kicked game show ass like some sort of *Hollywood Squares* ninja. Sticking to my training, I sailed through the first round, taking the game and five hundred dollars barely breaking a sweat. I felt unstoppable, adrenaline flowing like blood through my veins—I could practically smell my new leather interior—until, suddenly, without warning, Super Dave Osborne tried to screw me.

We were deep in the second game when I went to Super Dave to win. The host, John Davidson, read the question: "What causes the most household accidents: doors, stairs, or bicycles?" While Super Dave showed a pretaped bit where he performed a stunt he's known for, like getting shot out of a cannon or signing an autograph at an auto trade show, I tried to imagine exactly how a bicycle could cause a household accident. Were there people showing up in the ER because they'd been tooling around the master bedroom on a tenspeed and accidentally crashed into an armoire? This seemed like the least likely answer, so I was pretty sure it was either that or doors. I never once met a door I considered a trouble-maker. But then Super Dave said *stairs* and he sounded so positive about it that I went temporarily insane and agreed, even though it went against all my training.

Of course, the answer was doors. Bastard.

That square that didn't get the O left me open for a block, but luckily, my opponent didn't have my special ops training and lost the next question, leaving it wide open for me to take the square back. This time I did not fall for any Super Dave trickery, and I won the second game by sticking to my guns and not agreeing that as a child actor Shirley Temple made more money than Jackie Coogan or Mickey Rooney. That had to be false since who'd ever heard of Jackie Coogan? Sure enough, I was right.

Finally, the moment I'd been dreaming about for weeks was almost upon me. I was told to grab a key and choose one of five brand-spanking-new shiny Buicks positioned on the stage almost like a pyramid, which I would then get to try to start—right after the commercial break.

I went with my gut and chose the bright red Buick Sky-hawk right out in front like the first pin in a bowling triangle. The producers placed me behind the wheel of the car with my "good luck" celebrities. From watching the show, I was led to believe that the contestant got to choose which celebrities would come with her or him for moral support, but this was not the case. Garry Marshall was standing next to me, leaning against the car, which I had nothing against—I loved *Happy*

Days as much as the next girl. But, somebody named Andrea Evans was perched on top of *my* car like she was posing for a girlie calendar in a mechanic's garage. This didn't sit well with me, but I didn't have time to get truly riled up about how I would explain to my friends watching that I'm not gay or a soap opera fan and I had nothing to do with picking her because just then I noticed that the key I had in my hand wasn't even an actual car key. It was a skeleton key. I felt all the color drain from my face. This fake key clearly wasn't going to start the car which meant *I didn't win.* I'd already lost and now to add insult to injury I was supposed to sit there glowing like an expectant mother knowing I would not be leaving with my Skyhawk? It was almost too much to bear.

I didn't know what to do with the key, so I rolled down the window to ask Garry what he thought.

"Um, hey, Gar?"

"Yeah?" he answered in his heavy New York accent, clearly surprised at being addressed by a contestant.

"Look." I showed him the key. "This isn't even a real key. Do you know what I'm supposed to do with it?" Garry looked at the key, intently assessing the situation. The poor guy had no idea. He was just there to promote *Pretty Woman,* not to figure out the ins and outs of the game show business.

"Just fake it," was all he could come up with.

Fucking directors.

We came back from commercial and John Davidson boomed, "We're back with Stefanie and she's about to see if she won a brand-new Buick Skyhawk." Ha.

"Stefanie, start the car!" So I looked down at the ignition and did my best impression of someone starting a car. I figured if nothing else I should really try to sell my performance since Garry Marshall was watching and could possibly put me in his next movie. Then I sat waiting for a *wah wah waaah* noise. Instead, I heard some sort of sound effect that vaguely mimicked an engine turning over. But that was impossible. I was in the car and knew it definitely hadn't started. This was followed by balloons dropping from the ceiling and the audience cheering like they were in the front row of a Madonna concert. What was wrong with these people? Hadn't they ever seen someone lose on a game show before? That's when my new best friend Garry leaned in through the window.

"You won the car." And that's when I screamed. This was unbelievable! I'd really done it.

I vaguely recall filling out a bunch of legal paperwork with my name, address, Social Security number, and other information, presumably to get the "getting my new car" ball rolling. I was smiling so hard my face hurt, loving everyone like I was on ecstasy—"Good luck, cowboy!" I shouted when I saw that Big Red was making his way to the podium. "Go easy on Lisa!" I shouted to Tom who was sitting on a crate near the coffee table for the crew. Tom gave me the thumbs-up as if to say, "You done good, kid." I couldn't wait to get home and tell my mom she was off the hook.

Mom was nonplussed by my coup.

"Huh." It wasn't a question. "You simply won a car." Again, not a question.

"Yes, Mom. I won it. Isn't it exciting? Now you don't have to give me any money. I did this myself."

"What about the taxes? Does the show pay for that, too?" Had my mother always been this big a buzz kill? I wondered to myself. Come on, taxes? Taxes were for grown-ups. Adults with decent jobs and houses and things like that. The government was interested in people with money. They weren't wasting their time on twenty-one-year-old kids who went on game shows and won a car they sorely needed. My mom was so naïve.

A few weeks later, I took possession of my Skyhawk. It had no mileage! It also had no leather interior and no air-conditioning, because air-conditioning was three thousand dollars extra. "Yeah, no thanks. Just the car, please," I told the dealership when they called with the news about how much the additional things would cost. Who needed a cassette player anyway when there were perfectly fine FM/AM radio stations?

Now there was just the question of what to do with my yellow Mazda. At this point it was barely drivable. It also had about twenty unpaid parking tickets on it, which meant that if I just left it parked on the street it would eventually get towed away—a bit anticlimactic for a car that had been with me through so much. But I had no other choice. So I said my good-byes and within two days the car was gone.

The following year, I did receive a form from the government stating that I'd won around fourteen thousand dollars in cash and prizes. I round-filed it along with the letters I started receiving a few years later from the IRS. About five years later, the phone rang on a random afternoon.

"Hello?" Pause.

"I'm looking for a Stefanie Wimmer? This is the Internal Revenue Service calling about your outstanding bill of eight thousand dollars, which includes interest from the last five years."

"*Hola?*"

Chubz

When I saw the ad in the classified section of the paper, I knew it was for me:

"Would you like to make easy money in a relaxed environment with room for advancement?"

Um, let me think . . . yeah!

"Imagine a fun, creative job that offers flexibility and a weekly paycheck between $500–$1,200."

I think I'm in love! But not so fast. There's probably a catch.

"Great pay, great incentives in the exciting world of telemarketing!"

Perfect! I didn't know what telemarketing was *exactly*, but it sounded right up my alley. I loved talking on the phone and I loved marketing.

"Start tomorrow—have a check by Friday!"

Sold! The phone was in my hand in seconds and a few

minutes later I'd secured an interview for later that same day. I was optimistic. Seeing as I'd just put down stakes in a run-down apartment just off of Hollywood Boulevard with my best friend, Beth, solely on her dime, I needed a job fast. I'd started my cross-country trek from Massachusetts to my new life with nine hundred dollars cash—a lot of money to me at eighteen. But my funds went quickly on 7-Eleven Slim Jims and Motel Six stays. We'd started the trip with lofty plans to camp out in order to save money, but that strategy flew out the window after the very first time we spent two hours in a campground unsuccessfully trying to pitch our tent. We eventually ended up partially dozing in our car on the side of the road at 2 a.m., paranoid that we'd be raped by the truck drivers we'd brazenly been flashing for hundreds of miles. By the time a down payment was needed for the apartment, I was flat broke and it was up to Beth's Bat Mitzvah savings account to finance our new place and budding marijuana addiction.

When I told Beth about my golden opportunity, all she said was, "Be careful. Better make sure this thing is on the level." What was she even talking about? I might've only been living in Los Angeles for a week, and I might've, much to my consternation, still been a virgin, but I wasn't dumb. I'd seen a few movies of the week in my time. I knew about *Dawn: Portrait of a Teenage Runaway*. I'd heard about these young girls straight off the bus in Hollywood, immediately getting preyed upon by some pimp who wants them to pose for "modeling pictures" and BAM they're sucked into the seedy world of prostitution or pornography never to be heard from again. *"Très jolie, Coco. Très jolie."* Obviously, I was too smart to fall into that trap.

"It's a phone job. Telemarketing. I'm sure it's cool."

"I'm just saying, it might be a scam," Beth said just before sucking in a huge hit through a blue glass bong we'd received as a "welcome neighbor" gift from the guy in the apartment next door.

"I'll tell you the real scam: *Bat Mitzvahs.* Chant a little Hebrew for two hundred of your closest friends and family and everyone gives you so much money you never have to sling Whoppers at a Burger King for three months until you finally get moved up to cashier where you are eventually fired for routinely shorting customers a few cents on their change in a noble attempt to help raise your minimum wage."

Okay, perhaps I was a little bitter. Despite the fact that I was Jewish, my parents didn't seem to notice, celebrating Christmas every year until I was about twelve. Suddenly, out of nowhere, my mother remembered our heritage, joined a temple and forced me to attend Hebrew school, even though at this point there was no chance I'd be studying enough to have a Bat Mitzvah. She also put the kibosh on Christmas, leaving me irritated and broke at thirteen. But at least I knew the value of a dollar.

Later that day, a pleasant blond woman of about thirty who introduced herself as "Genie with a G" looked me up and down, and then asked me to read from a script to see how well I articulated over the phone. I never had a big interest in acting, but I *had* been chosen to play Dorothy in the local community center's production of *The Wizard of Oz* when I was in the second grade, so I knew it wouldn't be a problem. The script itself was one I'd know by heart within a few weeks.

"Hi, this is (insert your name here) from General Business Warehouse. You're on our preferred customer list, so I'm paying you a courtesy call to tell you about the huge savings I'm able to offer you *today only* on your office-supply needs. Am I speaking to the person who makes the purchasing decisions at your company?"

To no one's surprise, I was told I could start the next day.

But before leaving, I was led to a back office to be introduced to the owner of the company. I wished that Genie with a G had warned me of what I was about to see. Even just a minimal, "Hope you're not scared of a little chest hair" comment would've been helpful. But I never saw it coming. The door swung open and standing there was a humongous Hungarian version of Brando in his bloated final days. For a second I thought, *How cute, someone dressed up a bear in people clothes!* The bottom of the man's shirt was fiercely trying to fight free from the waistband of his pants and the buttons on his shirt were pulled so tightly I was afraid if one popped off someone could lose an eye—well, the few buttons that he'd actually buttoned. His shirt was purposely opened almost to his navel, exposing mounds of chest hair. It was a truly horrifying sight. But I didn't say anything.

First off, we were still a good twenty years away from

it being acceptable for a man to get his chest waxed—this was the eighties, call-waiting had yet to be invented, and many people were still under the impression that Kajagoogoo would have another hit. Second, he seemed downright proud to be hairier than a Cro-Magnon, and since this was the man who would be signing my weekly paycheck of $500–$1,200, I figured it best to keep my thoughts to myself. I smiled widely and tried to maintain eye contact despite the bowl haircut, gold tooth, and huge medallion, which were all equally battling it out for my attention. He stuck out a big meatloaf hand.

"I'm Chubz. Eez veddy, veddy nice doo meet you," he said in the thickest Hungarian accent since Zsa Zsa Gabor. "I hope doo be zeeing much more of you."

I hoped not.

The large room where I worked was lined wall to wall with cubicles. Genie with a G brought me over to an empty one and I was provided with a phone, order pad, a book of "leads," and my script.

"All of this is for me?"

"Yeah," said Genie with a G. "Have a seat and we'll get you started." Wow. It was straight out of the last scene in *Working Girl*! My very own desk and phone! I'd truly arrived!

My coworkers were a ragtag bunch: a couple of rocker types, a part-time Michael Jackson impersonator, a few actors, and a smattering of girls. The girls seemed to be mostly scantily clad fake blondes with big boobs. I wondered if wearing a tube top helped inspire the sales team somehow. It seemed like the girls spent most of their time chatting with each other about nightclubs and "how totally trashed" they'd gotten the night before, but I was determined to be a high earner. For approximately six hours a day, my job was to call people and get them to buy office supplies by any means necessary. Most calls went like this:

"Hi. This is Donna Kay (we got to make up fake names for ourselves and I thought Donna sounded very professional) from General Business Warehouse. You're on our preferred customer list, so I'm paying you a courtesy call to tell you about the . . . hello? Hello?" But within a few days I was able to keep people on the line a bit longer. After my opening, if they were still there, I attempted to take the customer straight to a yes.

"Now, are you still using those Scripto Deluxe ink pens? . . . Great! Why don't I just get a gross of those out to you." That was not said as a question. "And because you're ordering today I am authorized to send you a touch-tone phone with automatic redial. Would you like one in black, pink, or red?" This, of course, was just a regular cheapo phone with a redial button for people impressed by not having to re-press seven numbers, but I delivered it like I was offering to throw in a free cruise to Europe. I'd been given one of these phones to take home the first day I worked there, and the nine button had gotten stuck permanently on its maiden call.

"Just give me your personal address so I can make sure this phone gets delivered straight to your . . . I'm sorry, you're only a two-person office and that's too many pens you say? . . . No problem, let's just do a few dozen of the pens and get you set up with some writing pads. I have down here that you prefer the perforated edges."

If I felt a call going south after I'd already had them somewhat interested, I was supposed to hand them over to a "closer." The closers were a bunch of Chubz's cronies who didn't seem to have much to do other than eat extremely pungent seafood stews, discuss their rotisserie baseball teams all day, and play cards. But, they had the special ability to offer potential buyers a 25-inch color television set.

On Friday, after almost a week of calls that were mostly unproductive save for a couple that went to closers, I was called into Chubz's office, where I presumed I'd be handed my walking papers. Instead I was presented a check for five hundred dollars. "Keep up zee good work and next week you make more. Much more." I didn't even know what to say. I was giddy.

"Really? Because I didn't make any actual sales yet. I mean, I'm really close but . . ."

"I hear you make *many* sales. Eez veddy good."

"I did? I do?"

"You send calls to closers, they close. You are gifted girl."

"Oh, great! Thank you." I too saw huge star potential in myself in the field of telemarketing. I was just thankful Chubz had noticed.

"You have very large breasts."

"*Oh.*" This was also true, but it had never been pointed

out in such an offhand manner, so I didn't quite know how
to respond.

"I give you a television set." *Huh?*

"Oh, no, no. That's not necessary," I said, although
truthfully Beth and I had been going crazy because there'd
been no room in the car for a television and no money once
we arrived in LA. I figured I'd definitely be blowing my first
paycheck at Circuit City. But, there was no possible way I was
going to even entertain the notion of accepting a TV from
my new boss. I mean, sure, I may have been a natural at this
whole sales business, but wasn't it just a little premature to
reward me with a television?

"Don't vorry. I haf whole warehouse full of TV sets."

"No, Chubz, I absolutely cannot accept a gift like that.
But thank you so much for offering."

The next day, two men delivered a 25-inch color TV set
right to the door of my apartment. That night Beth and I
celebrated by getting high and watching *Small Wonder*—the
show about the ten-year-old robot girl—an extremely under-
rated show if you're stoned.

Monday morning I arrived at work bright and early
with a spring in my step. For me, a weekend spent doing
nothing more than reacquainting myself with favorite TV
shows was more rejuvenating than a forty-eight-hour foot rub
would be to someone else. Settling in at my desk, I felt more
determined than ever to move some merchandise and prove
Chubz right about me.

My very first call of the day, I explained to a patient old

woman that it was National Safety Week and first-aid kits were being offered for half price. That afternoon, Genie took me into her office to tell me I was invited to a mandatory Vegas trip set for the following weekend.

"Wow, is it some sort of sales conference?" I asked.

"Something like that," Genie with a G answered non-committally. "Bring something sexy to wear and a bikini."

Vegas. A mandatory invite. This was a bit odd. Confused, I went back to my cube, but before picking up the receiver to make my next call, I looked around the office. Two different girls in the office used the fake name Bambi. The strangeness of that hadn't occurred to me before just this moment. I interrupted a conversation about fake nails between Bambi #1 and a girl who went by Darla. "Are you guys going to the sales conference this weekend?"

Bambi #1 stared at me blankly. "Sales conference?" *Shit.* I instantly felt bad. Obviously, she hadn't been mandatorily invited to the conference and now I'd leaked it. It was probably only for the more successful telemarketers. I'd never seen Bambi make a call, let alone a sale.

"Never mind," I said as casually as if I'd just asked if she wanted a piece of gum and then realized I was all out. I picked up my receiver and put it to my ear.

"Are you talking about the photo shoot?" Bambi asked.

"In Vegas?" Darla added. Now I was really confused.

"Did Chubz call it a sales conference?" Bambi said, giggling. Was it possible that I was being laughed at by someone who purposely called herself Bambi?

"I didn't talk to Chubz. Genie just told me Vegas. What photo shoot?" I didn't want to sound dumb, but I had to know.

"Chubz brings the girls he likes to Vegas to model. I *know* you don't think we make twelve hundred a week selling pens." Bambi was definitely laughing now. Bitch. Chubz's words echoed back to me in my mind, sounding a lot more disgusting than they did at the time. *You'll make more. Much more.* My stomach was starting to feel a little unwell. The stench from the closers' office wasn't helping.

"Yeah, no, I didn't know there was any modeling involved." What kind of modeling exactly? I was grasping here, but I just really didn't want it to be true. I'd kind of been envisioning a successful future in sales and I wasn't quite ready to let it go yet.

"Oh, God, it's no biggie, there's no nudity! It's just topless," Darla offered, assuming she was being helpful. The only way I could see someone thinking topless modeling was no big deal would be if that person was used to doing something else . . . like bottomless modeling! How could I have not seen this coming? How could I have thought that making *no sales* was the sign of a sales savant?

"Oh, cool. Cool," I said as if I had conversations about nude modeling all the time, and I turned back to my phone so that no one could see my face. I tried really hard not to cry, but I felt so incredibly foolish—so ridiculous and gullible.

Was everything in LA like this? Did I always have to be on the lookout? Most important, did I have any talent in sales?

That night I reluctantly told Beth what happened. I might not have but she would've become suspicious when she found me in my pajamas all day eating bagels. I was fully expecting an "I told you so" or at least an appalled reaction. Instead she started laughing. Of course, she was a little high, but it still took the sting out of it. Before long I was laughing, too—possibly due to joining her in her drug abuse. But, really, it was pretty funny.

The next day I didn't show up for work. Or the day after that. In fact, I never went back.

At 6 a.m. the following Monday after the mandatory "sales conference" I'd been absent from, I awoke to a pounding on the door. Beth and I, both startled, met in the hallway and looked at each other wide-eyed. We tiptoed up to the peephole and peeked out. Standing in front of our door were two burly men with matching bowl haircuts. *What the hell?*

"Let uz in!" I grabbed the phone to call 911 but realized immediately that would be impossible due to the damn sticking #9. The pounding got even louder and the men outside started yelling. "Open up zis door. We come for Chubz's television set."

Damn. I really wanted that TV. And although it was a sleazy operation and one I wanted no part of, I still thought maybe I deserved the television.

Beth and I watched as the men walked down the long driveway with our beautiful television. "Stop!" I yelled. The men turned. "Here. Might as well take the phone, too."

I'm Free,
Freebasin'

When I was not quite twenty-one, I accidentally freebased cocaine. Sure, it seems a fairly unlikely thing to
happen accidentally—I know what people might think when
they read that: How do you accidentally freebase cocaine, an
illegal drug? Isn't it a bit like saying you accidentally ran down
your ex with your car in his driveway? So, I understand how
this could right from the get-go seem suspect. Add to that the
fact that cocaine is a highly illegal and expensive drug, so it's
not like "accidentally" devouring all the donuts in a business
meeting because they were just sitting there on the conference
table taunting you with their deliciousness until you just
suddenly went crazy and ate the whole box. Let's face it, rock
cocaine is rarely lying around a conference table—unless the
conference table is at a record company.

But one night, I, a nice Jewish girl from Forest Hills, New York, sat on my couch that smelled like cat pee even though we didn't own a cat, and smoked cocaine.

I'd snorted cocaine a handful of times at this point in my life. It was the eighties, and coke seemed about as dangerous as Molly Ringwald. It wasn't unusual for someone to whip out a little baggie of powder at a bar, roll up a ten-dollar bill, and go to town. I didn't often partake, mainly because when I do coke I feel amazing, self-confident, chatty yet genuinely interested in other peoples' lives . . . for the first twenty minutes and then I lose all the good-feeling part but remain nervous, hyper, and fearful. For the next six hours, I'm slightly less fun to have around than an untrained Pomeranian. Uppers and my high-strung personality have never been a good match. Twenty years later, it's only gotten worse. These days, I can't even take a single Sudafed without wanting to go on a killing spree. But back then I was young, cocaine was hip, and I really wanted to make my relationship with drugs work—so I kept giving it a go.

My roommate, Beth, was only seventeen when we arrived in Los Angeles. Her newfound freedom had spun her straight out of control and she never let something as trivial as "having a job" get in the way of a good time. It wasn't that she didn't work; she was spontaneous and not afraid to quit a job at the spur of the moment for another job with better pay or fewer hours. As a result, she'd been through quite a few gigs throughout our first year in Hollywood. The night we freebased, she'd been working in a clothing store on Melrose

Avenue for a couple of weeks. She and the assistant manager, Angela, a Swede with a set of startlingly great real breasts, didn't so much *work* at the store as much as they embezzled from the owners by intercepting new inventory, loading a ton of it into trash bags, hauling them outside to the trash, then pulling up in Angela's Jeep around 2 a.m. to retrieve the bags before the actual trash trucks came. Then they could sell the clothes for a major markdown to their friends, reaping a nice little profit, or keep what they liked for themselves.

As Beth became more and more radical, I found myself cowering in the opposite direction. Beth was seeking adventures and freedom from an oppressive upbringing, but I was looking to make a fresh start and find the security I lacked growing up. After a few crappy jobs, I found employment in a life insurance company as a clerk because I was under the impression that working for twelve grand a year in a stifling-hot office with coworkers who by and large only spoke Tagalog, the native language of the Philippines, would give me that stability I so craved. I thought this might also lead to a better credit rating and a little spending money, but so far the only thing it had added to my life was fifteen pounds, thanks to my cubicle's close proximity to the floor's vending machine.

The morning of the freebasing incident, I was in a hurry to get to work; they'd just hired a new hyper-strict supervisor fresh out of the United States Military Academy and I was afraid I might have to drop down and give him twenty if I dared to punch in thirty seconds late. As I was running for the door, I tripped over Beth's current boyfriend, Roo, who was passed out on the floor while Beth watched cartoons from the nearby couch. Roo was a portly goth with a penchant for wearing eyeliner, who'd been released from the Marines on a Section 8, which meant he was psychologically unfit for service—but apparently great boyfriend material if mental stability isn't high on your priority list.

"Damn it, Beth. Do you have to keep your boyfriends lying around on the floor where people can trip on them?" I bitched, while grabbing my car keys off the special hook I had on the wall labeled CAR KEYS.

"You know what? You are getting way too uptight!" Beth said, glaring at me from her perch. Although she was only about five feet tall and ninety pounds soaking wet, she still seemed kind of menacing with her pointy mohawk and the black monkey boots she loved to wear. That comment really stung since I'd always seen myself as the rebel. I mean, it was my idea to move to California, but with Beth being seventeen and me being a *full* year and a half older, I had tried to be the mother figure.

"Hey, someone's got to make the money around here. The toilet paper's not going to buy itself!" I caught sight of myself in the mirror next to the front door shortly after making that comment, with short, pouffy hair and puffy skin that due to daily fluorescent light exposure made me so pale I almost looked like a film negative. *Wow. I'm not headed in a good direction.* I also took in my long burnt orange skirt and matching blazer with lapels that had the wingspan of a falcon that I wore almost every day because I didn't have any other choices. I suppose Beth could've hooked me up with some stolen goods, but almost everything in her store featured skulls, which somehow didn't seem suitable for a job where a client might drop by to discuss the accidental death clause in their policy.

When I came home that evening from work, my apartment was full of people. My high school friend Abbie, who was fairly loose in high school but since had become a born-again Christian and now worked as a flight attendant for Delta, had a layover in LA and was crashing with us for fourteen hours before heading back to Dallas. Next, our neighbor Garth, an out-of-work actor, if you didn't count the "extra work" on *The Love Boat* he'd been bragging about (which I didn't—but he did—in a major way), popped by to see if we had any pot. "Dude, I need to mellow out. I came *this* close to getting an under five today." Garth, like most wannabe actors, paused for dramatic effect after using any phrase that had to do with acting, like "under five," leaving plenty of breathing room for someone to ask for a definition. When no request came, he continued on as if we hadn't heard about his close calls a million times before. "We were doing this scene where I was just talking on the Lido deck with another couple of extras. We weren't talking *out loud,* but we were doing our thing I learned at the Learning Annex class I took on being an extra, mouthing, 'peas and carrots, peas and carrots, peas and carrots' when all of a sudden, Laurel, casting director *extraordinaire,* motions to me and says, 'We need you, Garth.'"

"You know the Lido deck isn't a real place, right?" I didn't want to burst his bubble, but I honestly felt a little concerned for his safety out in the real world and I knew this was probably scaring Abbie. Instead I wanted to pull her into my room to gossip, but there was another knock at the door and in walks Angela's boyfriend, who looked a lot like a terrorist, although I'd never seen one up close before.

At this point, Abbie and I decided to make ourselves scarce, so I took off my blazer, threw on a Hands Across America sweatshirt, and we walked down to the corner 7-Eleven for beef jerky and cherry Slurpees, hoping everyone would have cleared out by the time we got back.

Returning a little while later to the apartment, I'm not sure what was more discomfiting: the smell of cat pee (which Beth and I just couldn't get used to), the smell of some other drug burning, or the Nick Cave and the Bad Seeds album playing at a level usually reserved for outdoor arenas.

"Guys, come on, we're smoking up," the Terrorist said as casually as if he was calling us kids to the dinner table. Abbie and I sat down on the couch and the Terrorist took a huge hit and then passed it over to Abbie. I looked at Abbie, fully expecting her to leap up and give an impromptu sermon or at the very least a Bible quote to fit the situation, but she nonchalantly took the pipe and pulled in the smoke. I guess the New Testament doesn't explicitly talk about "no freebasing" so she was good as far as her faith was concerned.

The pipe was passed to me, but I only took one small hit, knowing cocaine was not always kind to me. I didn't want to get out of control. Who knew if smoking it would make it stronger? Within five seconds, I was flying higher than the Goodyear blimp. I was so high—like *holy crap* high. All sorts of crazy, speedy thoughts zipped through my head like lightning striking—so damn genius but so darn fleeting, I could only watch them flash by without being able to write it down or even share it with anyone. If I could've harnessed the high, I'm pretty sure I could've penned a best-selling novel in less than ten minutes or at least read one.

"Freebasing is the only way to do coke," the Terrorist said as he exhaled a lungful of toxic vapors.

This was 1986, so it was well after Richard Pryor had spent six weeks at a burn center after freebasing cocaine and then accidentally lighting himself on fire while doused with Bacardi 151. But (a) Up until that moment I didn't know what we were doing was freebasing. And (b) Even if I had known, I still probably wouldn't have worried about Richard Pryor's bad outcome because, clearly, if you're going to free-base cocaine, you have to use common sense and not just go dousing yourself with Bacardi or other flammable liquids. And it's probably best to stay indoors. That way, if there is trouble, the fire department has an actual address to shoot for and not just "find the guy running down the street on fire." But it was still clear that what we were doing wasn't exactly mainstream drug use.

Before I knew it, the fun buzz had worn off and I was passed the pipe again, so I did another hit, which was very possibly not the best idea given my low tolerance. I felt my jaw go completely rigid. My brain was still speeding along, thinking about a thousand thoughts a second, but I couldn't feel my hands or face and since my jaw was sort of paralyzed, I couldn't talk. Plus, the palpitating in my chest was so loud it was tough to concentrate on anything besides the fact that *I was surely on the verge of a heart attack.* Many years later, thanks to my medical training that consisted of watching every episode of *ER,* I diagnosed myself retroactively with tachycardia, the only cure for which is to *stop freebasing cocaine immediately.* Beth, Angela, Garth, and another random neighbor whose name I didn't even know but who clearly had a sixth sense when drugs were in the vicinity were howling at some story Garth had just told about Gopher. They were sipping beer and smoking cigarettes like nothing was out of the ordinary, while I sat like a frozen statue—a monument to all that could go wrong when smoking illegal drugs. *I never realized that I hate Garth. He's phony and has weird bangs and he's a damn extra, but the way he talks you'd think he gets picked up for work by a limo every day.*

Above the din in my head, I heard Beth talking excitedly about all the great money-making possibilities of becoming a coke dealer. *Really? Turn our apartment into a coke den? What was wrong with her?* Obviously, Beth was completely delusional if she thought being a coke dealer would be a simple career move. It seemed to me that besides being illegal, it would involve an awful lot of travel and she didn't have a car or even a pager for that matter.

I looked over at Beth, with her bags of stolen clothes in

the closets and dreams of selling drugs, and had the realization that I was going to have to move out of this apartment if I was to have any chance of not spending the rest of my life in a federal penitentiary.

Normally, *I* was the bad influence on other people and I felt fairly confident about my role, but my bad influence went about as far as coaxing people into talking back or making crank phone calls—not selling crank! I was barely out of my teens, freebasing cocaine in my living room. And, hell, I wasn't even a starlet dealing with the high pressure of becoming America's sweetheart because my sitcom suddenly blew up and now I was getting two tons of fan mail every day and paparazzi were camped outside my door and there was no way to relieve the intense pressure except heavy drug use. I was doing data entry.

Even though all I wanted to do was sit and grit my teeth, I felt I should look for Abbie, whom I realized hadn't been in the room for quite a while. I hoped she wasn't in a shame spiral, her head buried in the Good Book or, worse, praying to the porcelain god. But I needn't have worried. She was in my bedroom in a full-on grope session with the Terrorist— aka, Angela's *boyfriend.* They both looked up but continued what they were doing, like humping dogs who had no idea they were doing anything wrong. I wondered momentarily if I should intervene, but luckily, the Terrorist got up, adjusted his pants, and left the room.

Abbie and I laid in my bed, avoiding conversation, and tried to fall asleep, but since even snorting one line of coke can keep me up for four days it wasn't happening. I would need something to come down—like maybe fourteen Valium. Abbie and I tossed and turned for a while when suddenly the door to my room burst open and the Terrorist was back standing there looking like he'd just stumbled into the cockpit of a plane and was ready to reroute us to Brisbane.

"Where is it?" he yelled. He was sweating profusely and looked incredibly suspicious.

"Where's what?" I asked, knowing full well I'd have no idea what he was talking about.

"Where's the rock? One of you stole it. Where the fuck is it, you bitches?" Wow, now that was rude. Drug dealer or not, he was a guest in our home.

"Obviously, I didn't steal your coke seeing as you had your hand down my pants until fairly recently," Abbie said matter-of-factly. *Thanks, Abbie. Real holy of you.*

"So that leaves you," the Terrorist said, pointing a hairy finger in my direction. "Which makes sense since you're still wide-awake."

"I'd still be awake if I had a half cup of coffee. This proves nothing. I think you need to leave."

"I'll tell you what I'm going to do. I'm going out to my car to get my gun and then we'll see if you can figure out where my rock went." I grabbed the phone to call 911, but before dialing I thought of how this was all going to look to the police. I didn't imagine I looked like the picture of innocence at that point. *How could a night of freebasing cocaine go so wrong?*

Just then Angela walked in.

"Shut up," she said to the Terrorist. "He's not going to do anything. He's just really paranoid. He's harmless." *Yeah, isn't that what most people say about their pit bulls moments before they rip some unsuspecting toddler's larynx out?*

And just like that, everyone left. And a month later, I moved to the San Fernando Valley into an apartment with a roomie I met on Roommates.com. Turned out she did a lot of coke, too.

Recently, I spoke to Beth on the phone. We remained friends through the years and still email all the time. She is a fun, normal mom of two who lives in a log cabin in Vermont with her husband. She's been known to bake a pie.

"Hey, Beth, remember when we freebased coke that one time? And that crazy guy threatened to kill us 'cause he thought I stole his rock of cocaine?"

"*Oh my God.* Right. You know what's really funny? Angela and I had found the rock in the carpet and totally smoked it."

"Huh." *Jesus, I was lucky to be alive. Oh, well.* "Yeah, pretty hilarious, I guess." And then I went back to finishing the fairies jigsaw puzzle I was working on with my four-year-old daughter.

Any Given Sunday Dad

Life is like an onion. The outer layers are a joke, and when you peel them away, there's another joke underneath. And underneath that yet another joke, and underneath that yet another. When you get to the core of the onion, however, it's no joke.

—STANLEY MYRON HANDELMAN

The earliest memory I have of my father is seeing him on television when I was about three. It was probably *The Ed Sullivan Show* or *Dean Martin*. I waved at the TV, which I recall my mother found hilarious and she wasn't an easy laugh.

"Hi, Daddy! Here I am! Daddy!" I looked to my mom, demanding to know why I wasn't getting his attention. In fact, he seemed engrossed in a conversation with a couple other people that annoyingly didn't include me.

"He can't see you, sweetie." I didn't know how that was

possible. I was right in front of him—yelling. And it was highly probable that I was naked and dancing. Looking back, it's a good thing I wasn't in the studio audience.

My father was on talk shows a lot when I was small— too small to actually know what a talk show was. When I heard "talk show," the image it brought up was a group of great minds talking together like a think tank—I thought my father was part of a team of very important people choosing a new president or discovering a hidden planet. I had no idea that he was doing something way more difficult: he was telling jokes. Later, I found out that my father was a comedian and he was almost famous. Not quite there yet but definitely on the cusp, performing regularly on *Merv Griffin*, *The Smothers Brothers*, *Ed Sullivan*, even opening for Frank Sinatra in Vegas. I came along with my parents for one of his Sinatra gigs and my mother and I stayed holed up in our hotel room while my father ate spaghetti with homemade Ragu sauce with Frank and his posse after the show. Even though my father and his on-stage persona was classic nerd (Greek fisherman's hat, big glasses, a slightly hunched-over posture, and goofy delivery), this was old school, men's club Vegas and wives were definitely not welcome.

Eventually, he headlined Caesar's Palace, which was quite the coup for a comedian known for subtlety at a time when most jokes ended with "Ba Da *Boom!*"

My father wasn't a household name, but he was famous enough that when I moved away from Los Angeles to Spokane, Washington, when I was twelve, my junior high school

teachers thought it was "cool" when they discovered my co-
medic pedigree. "Oh, sure, I know who your dad is!" they'd
say excitedly. "What was it like growing up with a comedian?
It must've been so . . . funny! I bet he was constantly telling
jokes!"

"Oh, well, I didn't really grow up with him but, yeah,
he's a funny guy." Sadly, fascination with my father never
translated into better grades.

My parents divorced when I was four. My father was
hitting his stride in the joke-telling biz, so with his wife out
of the picture he did what anyone who's made a few appearances on talk shows and knows he's on the brink of "very big
things" does—he relocated to a bachelor pad smack dab on
the beach in Malibu. This wasn't the Malibu of *90210* lame
bonfire parties where Jennie Garth's character might lose her
virginity to the tune of a Color Me Badd ballad; this was the
groovy *Love, American Style* Malibu circa the early seventies
where anything goes.

My father had the requisite sponger friends (one with a
huge mustache who could do a standing backflip), a throng
of bikini-clad neighbors often running around with the top
part removed, and he always had a small dog—usually a
Chihuahua—that went with him everywhere. He was like
the original Paris Hilton—if Paris Hilton looked like Woody
Allen and could speak in complete sentences. Meanwhile, I
lived first in a few one-bedroom apartments and then eventually in a two-bedroom duplex in a highly questionable part of
town. My father became an occasional Sunday dad. I looked

forward to his appearances but definitely couldn't count on them. He often had big plans to come and take me for the day but mostly couldn't make it happen. Many times he had a migraine and called at the last minute to say he was not up to it. Sometimes he didn't call at all and I waited by our front window looking for his car until it was undeniable that he wasn't coming. But, in those days, when he did show up, it was all the more special.

We had our place, The Shrimp Boat, a seafood stand on the ocean that served fried shrimp with the tails still on in a long porcelain dish shaped like a boat, which I munched happily, leaving not a crumb of breading on my plate. Of course, I now realize that crunching down a shrimp tail has as much glamour and about the exact same sound as biting down on a cockroach. But when I was with my father, I didn't want to leave anything behind. Sometimes we'd get a whole steamed crab that the cooks dropped into a huge vat of boiling water right in front of our eyes. My father showed me how to crack open the shell and get to the meat inside, separating the green stuff from the rest of the prize.

People constantly approached my father for his autograph. I didn't understand why anyone would want my father to write his name on a piece of paper for them. He was always fractured, an absentminded professor type, but he lit up when people wanted a picture, an autograph, or a bit of his presence. My time with him was so limited that although it was interesting at first to watch a couple in matching Santa Monica Pier sweatshirts go crazy over my dad, I began to resent the strangers who were taking up the little time and piece of my father I had left.

Sometimes we went to fancy restaurants where I wore outfits handsewn by my mother who couldn't afford to buy me new clothes, and my father ordered me frog's legs—a delicacy apparently enjoyed by French people, rich people, and people who will eat anything that comes from a pond.

"Come on, try it. It tastes like chicken." I'd eat it to please him. And it was true that it tasted like chicken. But, I thought, then why not just order chicken? And while you're ordering chicken, go ahead and make it chicken nuggets because chicken nuggets are seriously delicious.

When I was about nine, my father moved to a modest apartment on Robertson Boulevard, closer to the place I then shared with my mother, stepfather, brother, and newborn sister. His career hadn't taken off like he'd been sure it would and our visits became even more infrequent. When we did get together, his tone started out jovial. He loved nothing more than to tell me jokes and recite lines of his act for me, such as: *I just had a very long accident. I was at the mall and I fell down the up escalator for about an hour and a half.* Even if I'd already heard them, I always laughed like it was the first time. His talent was awesome to me. But not long into our visit, he would usually roll into bitterness at the business. "These goddamn bookers are a bunch of thieves—not to mention the agents and managers. Have you seen me on *Merv*? I kill 'em every time." He was usually in a feud with someone or other, but I didn't know the players well enough to weigh in one way or another.

My mother told me that my father burned a lot of bridges. "He alienates people," she'd say when I'd complain that my father didn't have friends.

One Sunday, he took me to play tennis at the local park. I wasn't exactly a sports-oriented kid. In fact, I was pretty horrendous, uncoordinated, and self-conscious with almost any activity that involved a ball, court, or field. If I was ever forced to take part in a team sport, the very last thing you'd hear from me is "Hey, coach, put me in!" The one and only time I was forced to play softball as a kid, I was sent far out to right field where I prayed that no ball would come within a city mile from my position. Of course, one did, and of course, I missed it and stumbled around like a drunken donkey trying to find the ball and throw it to someone, anyone—which in my blind panic ended up being someone from the opposing team. To this day, I will go to great lengths to avoid public sports humiliation. Invitations to join Jack and Jill softball leagues, bowling teams, and beach volleyball games are met with the same panicked response: "Love to, but this restless leg syndrome's got me sidelined for a while—just waiting on a cure!"

On the tennis court, my father lobbed a few balls at me that zoomed straight by my head or bounced sloppily off my racket, leaving me running after them and leaving him frustrated. I think he could tell his frustration was making my playing worse, so he tried to distract me with small talk.

"What grade are you in now?"

"Um, fourth?" *Hello!*

Even at the age of nine I understood that when your own father has to ask you what grade you're in it's a pretty good tip-off you aren't close.

"Your father doesn't relate well to children," my mother told me on more than one occasion when I came home sad and disappointed with my failure to connect with him. "Things will probably be different when you're an adult. He'll be able to really have conversations with you then."

My father's favorite kind of music was jazz. To say I'm not a jazz fan would not do my dislike of it justice. I'm pretty sure I'd rather sit through a round of chemotherapy than a full record of experimental or improvisational jazz. It's a lot like modern art—how do they know if it's unbelievably genius or could be re-created by a monkey? There's no melody, no lyrics. How do these "musicians" even name their songs? It's always struck me that pop musicians will spend hours writing a song that lasts for three minutes. Yet jazz musicians will spend three minutes coming up with a song that goes on for hours. But my father believed that jazz was brilliant. He loved nothing more than to roll a joint with a small device that reminded me of a miniature old-fashioned clothes wringer and burn daylight together listening to those endless songs. I'd try to sit still and force myself to learn to like it because sophisticated people like jazz—they understood it. I figured it might be an acquired taste like eating mayonnaise with French fries. Or frogs legs.

"How about a glass of OJ?" he'd ask absently after an hour and a half of straight jazz uninterrupted by needless chitchat because he didn't want to miss a G chord, which I assumed was probably played accidentally anyway.

"You and I, we're just alike. Two peas in a pod," he'd say sometimes. I knew it wasn't true; that he was only seeing what he wanted to see, not a jazz-hating, sports-sucking, unfunny fraud.

My mother was his third wife and he wasn't yet on marriage number four. Sometimes when we saw each other he told me that he felt so lucky to have me as a daughter because I was the only one who really got him. With all the people constantly screwing him over, he said I was his only real friend, the only person he could trust.

So when he was seriously injured after getting hit by a car, I cried not just because he was hurt but from the weight of it. I cried because he said no one was coming to visit him while he lay in a hospital bed recuperating from a broken hip, arm, leg, ribs, and head trauma. He did, in fact, have three sons from his first two marriages, but I didn't really know who they were or if he was even in touch with them, so I begged my mother and stepfather to please go see him because he had no one. So they did. He asked them to bring him a boom box so he could listen to the healing sounds of Chick Corea and a bunch of other essentials like chocolate, pistachio nuts, books, and "this dynamite extra-aged Gouda I absolutely love from a little store in Westwood"—and my mother and stepfather obliged. Not for him, but for me.

Much later, he wrote a joke about the incident: "I was in a terrible accident. I was walking along the sidewalk minding my own business when I was hit by a mobile library truck. I was lying in the street moaning and crying in pain. Finally, the driver leaned out of the window and said, 'Shhhhh!'"

I always thought that was one of his funniest.

A couple of years later, my family moved to Washington State. My father didn't call much or write and I never saw him, but when people asked about him or knew who he was, I always said proudly, "Yes, that's my father." A few years after that, we moved again—this time across the country to Massachusetts. He was in his fifties now with a new wife in her early twenties and a new baby. I called to tell him I was moving. He ranted about his dislike of government, why we should all refuse to pay taxes (this was way before Wesley Snipes made it cool), and his high esteem for the Communist system. I wasn't used to keeping my opinions to myself anymore and he wasn't used to me expressing anything but awe, so we ended up in an argument. The call ended on a slightly sour note.

I didn't see him or talk to him for the next three years that I lived on the East Coast, although I'd often go out drinking with my friends, come home, and scrawl him a long letter about how much I missed him, how horrible things were with my parents, and how I wanted to come live with him— luckily, I didn't have his address since he'd moved again. It was the written version of drunk dialing—it included the hangover but saved me from "damage already being done." In retrospect, it's a great thing I didn't have a phone number for him anymore because unresolved feelings plus poor impulse control plus access to a telephone is a recipe for humiliation.

When I turned eighteen and moved back to Los Angeles, I became intent on finding him. With no phone number or address (and knowing he was long since divorced *again*), I resorted to scouring the *LA Weekly* and finally found him listed in the paper performing at a local comedy club/jazz venue, The Alley Cat Bistro.

I stood in the back of the room mesmerized by his performance. He commanded the stage, deliberately and slowly setting up his joke so that the sly punch line snuck up on you like waking up on your birthday with a gift at the foot of your bed. The crowd was in the palm of his hand and their reaction juiced him up as he rode higher and higher on their energy. Even after all these years, his timing was impeccable.

He walked through the crowd afterward flush with approval, shaking hands with audience members. I waited for him to walk by me, my heart beating faster than a ferret despite the three Sea Breezes I'd downed for courage. "That was great!" I said as he passed by. He stuck out his hand to shake with mine, the fan, one of many, who was here to compliment, pay homage.

"Thanks. Thanks a lot." He smiled.

He didn't recognize me.

He would've kept moving, but I forced myself to push on. "Uh, hey, do I look familiar?" I didn't want to scare him, but it wasn't like I'd hired a private detective to look up my long-lost birth parents who'd given me up for adoption when they were seventeen and I was now paying them a surprise visit at their family farm in Muskogee. It hadn't been *that* long since he'd seen me.

He smiled again. The exact same smile. He definitely had no idea who I was.

"It's me, Stefanie, your daughter." The relief on his face was palpable. But it wasn't relief to see me, finally. It was relief that his memory was no longer put on the spot.

"Stef! Heya! Great to see you! Great to see you!" A bleach blonde in her early thirties wearing a purple sequined top— the type of top usually reserved for alcoholic women in their sixties sitting at blackjack tables—sidled up to my father and slung an arm proprietarily around his waist.

"Hello, there," she purred. "Who's this?"

"This is my daughter, Stef. I haven't seen her in quite a few years." Was it my imagination or did it take him a beat too long to come up with my name? "This is my friend Kelly," he said, gesturing to Purple Sequins. Kelly was clearly caught completely off guard by this information. She made that face women make when they discover they've accidentally been drinking a regular Coke instead of Diet. But she recovered a split second later, like she was in a pageant.

"Well, hello!" Then Miss Congeniality looked at my father and hit him playfully on the arm. "You didn't tell me you had a daughter!" I really wished I hadn't just shown up. This was a mistake. But my father was enjoying it, walking me around introducing me to everyone in sight. "This is my daughter, Stefanie. Isn't she a beaut?"

An hour later I found myself at a table with him catching

him up on my years in Springfield. When the bill came for the appetizer we'd ordered, he looked sheepish. "Heya, Stef, would you mind getting this one?" I expected this from a first date but not from my Sunday Dad. I looked at him and really took it in. He looked older and sadder than I'd ever seen him. But at the same time, I felt strongly that he didn't know he was older and sadder—because he'd always made excuses for himself and obviously still did. I really didn't have any money either, but I took care of the bill. "Hey, thanks a lot. Next time, it's on me. By the way, is there any way I could borrow twenty bucks? I owe this guy in the band for a little weed."

I didn't have twenty bucks. I gave him ten.

"Thanks, again. I'm good for it. God, look at you, Stef, you're funny and smart and good-looking. You turned out just like me." He laughed at his own joke. "Listen, I really want to take you to this great little jazz club called The Money Tree. I want to be close."

I finally got it. The thing I hadn't gotten all these years. I didn't need him. He just needed me.

"We're really not that much alike, Dad," I said. "For starters, I actually don't like jazz."

Hitting the Bee

I broke my therapy cherry at the tender age of seventeen. My first therapist's name was Irma and she was maybe sixty. I wasn't an excellent judge of age at that point despite the fact that Botox was years away, but besides the wrinkles, I had a few hints; the woman was wearing bifocals and the most useless clothing item ever invented—a shawl—so that was a good tip-off that she was probably eligible for the senior citizen discount. I worried that a woman in her sixties wouldn't be able to relate much to a teenager's problems, but I tried to keep an open mind.

I was having "food issues" as well as "I hate my stepfather issues," not to mention that I could not go on more than two dates with a guy without feeling suffocated and things were not going well at home. I was a simmering stew of teen angst, anxiety, and anger. My mother, who was a mental health professional, felt strongly that counseling could cure everything from multiple personalities to third-degree burns. Maybe I should have known better than to consider her advice as gospel, considering my less than functional upbringing, but hindsight is 20/20 and, given the time I've spent in therapy, hindsight would have saved me enough cash over the years to be driving a Bentley Continental home to my own Neverland Ranch—but minus the llama. So my mother made the decision that I needed help—in fact, she made it a condition of my staying at home that I go talk to someone about why I couldn't get along with my stepfather.

Besides being about five generations away from me and reminding me not so slightly of a cafeteria lunch lady, Irma's bifocals magnified her eyes to such a cartoonish size that when she looked at me quizzically over the nearsighted top half, it made me think of one of those creepy big-eyed kid lithographs. It was disconcerting, to say the least. But the real deal breaker was that Irma was more than pleasantly plump and, unlike me, didn't seem to be agonizing over it in the least. She'd long ago given in to the allure of polyester pantsuits, and who could blame her? The woman was probably not packing up after a long day of doling out compassionate nods and hitting the nightclub circuit; she was more likely going home to rearrange her Hummel figurines and knit a tea cozy. How was I possibly going to tell her that eating two cookies made me feel like I may as well get in the car and hit every fast-food joint within a five-mile radius *because, fuck it, I'll always have a huge ass and no self control!* without having to add, "Not that there's anything wrong with that!"

My appointments were every Saturday morning and they usually followed a Friday night keg party, which brought with it a mean hangover, so most sessions I spent running back and forth to the bathroom or begging for Tylenol. Luckily, most of the time I saw her was during flu season so she didn't think too much of it. But I didn't start getting along with my stepfather any better, either.

Once I turned eighteen, I left the house and set out on my own, thinking I'd feel relief starting fresh. But instead of feeling a whole lot better as I'd expected, my anxieties intensified and with them my incessant ice cream eating and I could barely tolerate dating at all. It seemed maybe I should give therapy another go. Seeing as I had no health insurance and my options were limited, I found myself a therapist straight out of grad school who agreed to see me on a sliding scale— like at the bottom of the scale. I don't know if it was Ginger's newness to the field or just a personality disorder, but she was so friendly and eager she could've moonlighted as a cocker spaniel. I found myself spilling my guts to her right away— telling her all about my highly dysfunctional upbringing and sparing no ugly details. Unfortunately, I quickly discovered she was way too huggy. Any sad story I shared caused her to pop up from her chair like a jack-in-the-box and race around the coffee table that held her herbal tea and a tissue box to wrap me up in what she must've thought was a "safe feeling" hug. It was utterly horrifying and did nothing to help with my fear of intimacy, let alone my food issues.

To distract myself from her aggressive boundary crossing,

I would flip through my mental Rolodex of Ben & Jerry's ice cream flavors and concentrate on which one I would be buying the second my session wrapped up. I forced myself to see Ginger for another few weeks even though the more she teared up hearing about my past, the more shut down I became until I realized I was deliberately keeping things light because I didn't want to make Huggybear sad. I hated to admit defeat, but it was time to move on before I pushed Ginger to the edge.

I went through a quick succession of metal health "experts": one who made elaborate designs out of straws while eyeing a candy dish that sat on a table next to my couch as if the candy were in therapy and not me. Every so often she'd stand up without warning, reach across the table, make a grab for a piece of candy, sit back down, battle furiously with the wrapper until finally setting it free, and pop it into her mouth, all the while saying, "Go on, go on. I'm listening." It probably shouldn't have come as a complete shock to me when she had to cancel a session because she'd somehow managed to scratch her cornea with a potato chip.

An honorable mention for weirdness has to go to Cowl-Neck Sweater Queen, who, for some unknown reason, in every session wore an enormous cowl-neck sweater. I diagnosed her with either OCD, terrible fashion sense, or constant unsightly hickeys. Finally, I had a one-session-stand with a woman who listened to me intently for about ten minutes, and then without saying a word, walked to her closet and came out with a stuffed bumblebee and a whiffle ball bat. It wasn't clear whether these were items she just had lying around the house or if it was a kit she'd specifically picked up at Anger Issues R Us, but I didn't like where she seemed to be heading.

"I want you to take this bat and hit the bee with it."

"No. That's not really my thing. I thought maybe we could just . . . you know, talk."

"Stefanie. You have anger issues. The bee is here to help release your rage in a safe way." I was definitely having rage at that point; rage that she had the nerve to charge my insurance $125 dollars an hour for this. "Come on, pick up the bat and smack that bee!"

"Maybe I could just talk with the bee rationally?"

"Hit it!" And with that, she gave me a demonstration and whacked that bee so hard, so many times, I wondered if it would take out a restraining order.

"Your turn!" I barely made out her saying to me as I was letting myself out into the lobby.

For a while it seemed that maybe I could survive on self-help books alone. I bought them up by the shelfful and tried to heal myself from my bouts of anxiety and depression. I read *Feeling Good: The New Mood Therapy, Women Who Love Too Much, Struggle for Intimacy,* and *Women Who Don't Love Football But Are Unfortunate Enough to Love Men Who Love Women Who Love Football so They Have to Pretend.* Some of the books did bring up some good points but $12.95 rarely bought the real change I was looking for— which eventually left me back with my old friend therapy. Sitting on a couch and talking about myself for fifty minutes still sounded great in theory and I didn't want to let a handful of bad experiences cause me to shelve the whole project, but it seemed that so far my luck with therapists was not good. I did have friends in therapy and, sure, I could have asked a few of them for referrals, but a lot of my friends in therapy at the time seemed just as crazy as when they started.

My last head shrinker was named Thelma, another recent grad from a school that judging from her blatant disregard for professionalism was probably an online university. I smelled trouble from our very first session. She launched into a story about a case she was working on—tearing up along the way. I made a feeble attempt to comfort her while glancing at my watch and seeing my session ticking away.

Usually in a therapist's office, there's a clock positioned conveniently behind the client's head so the therapist can feel free to clock watch while trying to seem like she's making eye contact, sort of like a newscaster reading a teleprompter. This way, even if you've just worked up the courage to talk about the pivotal moment when your trusted high school drama coach asked if you'd care to witness his private performance of Puppetry of the Penis, when the clock hits the fifty-minute mark, the therapist will say, "I'm sorry. We're out of time today. How's next Tuesday at four?"

I knew this wouldn't be a problem with Thelma. She had a worse sense of time than a rock. An hour and a half crawled by before we both finally ran out of issues and I got to leave.

In my second session with Thelma, after the first twenty minutes discussing her problems, we finally got around to talking about me and she made a diagnosis: turned out, according to her, I was hilarious and the only trouble was that I needed to find the right guy. And she just happened to know one right at the hospital where she worked.

"He's in his fifties, just got divorced, and he has two kids. He's a super nice guy." No matter that he was twice my age, had kids, and, oh yeah, was her *colleague*. There are only like a hundred shades of wrong about that but maybe she was having Internet issues the day that class was taught.

"I don't think I'm ready for kids yet," I said.

"Well, we can work on that."

Thelma was obviously crazy as a crab cake, but it was clear she needed me at this point more than I needed her. Maybe to prove to myself that I didn't have commitment issues, I still stuck around for a couple more sessions.

On Valentine's Day, I broke down in the middle of my session—possibly from the dismal feeling of being in therapy on Valentine's Day and not ringing in the holiday by pouring chocolate fondue over some lover's private parts before soaking in the oversize Jacuzzi in our five-star hotel room in Paris. In the midst of my crying jag, I noticed a shadowy figure crouching outside the French doors of Thelma's office. It was easy to see since the doors were only covered with a flimsy nonsoundproofed set of gauzy white curtains.

"Someone's lurking outside your office!" I said, trying to stop a possible murderer or, worse, an eavesdropper. Thelma went to the door, opened it, and then crouched down to retrieve something.

"Oh, my goodness! What a sweetie pie!" she said, walking back in with a huge bouquet of roses. "It was my husband. He dropped by and left me these flowers for Valentine's Day. Anyhoo, you were saying how hard it is to find love and how sad Valentine's Day makes you feel . . ."

"Yeah."

"Hmmm." Placing her massive display of flowers on her desk, Thelma began straightening and arranging them.

"You know, my husband and I don't actually live together. I really think that's the secret to making a marriage work. Separate apartments. Are you surprised?" I couldn't have been less surprised considering I found her difficult to be around for ten minutes. What *did* surprise me, however, was that I was now pulling out my checkbook to pay *her*! Except that while I was writing out the check, I had a realization—a breakthrough if you will. It occurred to me that in a long series of fifty-minute increments I had found out plenty about myself. I was simply not nearly as dysfunctional as I'd thought. I mean, just compared to Thelma I was way ahead of the game. I felt such relief at this realization that tears welled up in my eyes.

Suddenly, Thelma pulled out one long-stem red rose and handed it to me.

"Here, Stefanie. I really want you to have this. You deserve it."

"Thanks, Thelma. But I'm afraid our time's up," I said as gently as I could. I hoped she could find herself a good therapist. I knew how hard it was.

It Works
If You Work It

Like almost every girl born and raised in the United States, I've never been happy with my body. In high school I found myself at a crossroads: be content in my size 11 jeans . . . *or* develop a raging eating disorder. One day, after a particularly filling Thanksgiving leftovers gorge, I discovered out of desperation that I could stick my finger down my throat and *voilà!*, no more sickly full feeling and no more guilt over the gazillion calories in mashed potatoes and gravy shoveled in whopping spoonful after spoonful. There is some mystery ingredient in mashed potatoes that makes all ugly feelings magically float away on a cloud of whipped butter, sweet carbs, and fairy dust only to crash back down to earth two days later and promptly land on your ass. If you don't believe me, just ask Oprah.

The problem was, I was petrified of getting fat but I loved to eat. The solution to my problem seemed too simple and vaguely dangerous, but I comforted myself in the knowledge that millions of sorority girls can't be wrong. And so I did it again. And again. It's not like I didn't consider other options: diet and exercise seemed way too time-consuming—being in my teens, I was in a bit of a time crunch—and anorexia was completely out of the question because I was *way* too lazy to starve myself. In fact, I felt the anorexics were really missing the boat on this shortcut. I laughed in the face of their carrot stick for breakfast, hollowed-out bagel for lunch, and Diet Coke for dinner. Amateurs.

Despite my Jewish heritage, no one in my immediate family, besides me, was the slightest bit obsessed with food or their weight. In fact, the opposite was true. My mother, a product of the seventies *Our Bodies, Ourselves* generation, was most comfortable walking around completely naked or in her underwear—in true hippie fashion, she'd never shaved her pits or anywhere else for that matter but had no self-consciousness hanging around a public pool, even though what was peeking out from her bathing suit could give Jerry Garcia's beard a run for its money. But, most important, she never made a single disparaging remark about my eating habits or figure. Yet I still fell into the trap of trying to control my life by controlling my body.

By the time I moved to Los Angeles, the city of skinny dreams, I was no longer a tourist in Bulimiaville—I'd established full-time residency and I knew I wasn't headed down a good path. I used food as my primary method of numbing out, spending my days fantasizing about what foods I'd eat later, alone in my apartment, the way other people might daydream about a party or a second date with a cute guy.

After work I'd head to the grocery store to pick up my stash. While in line with my treasures (a huge triangle of double cream Brie, Cherry Garcia ice cream, Jell-O instant pudding, Chips Ahoy!, and a bag of baby carrots—to throw judgmental looky-loos off my trail), I'd make up a little story in my head for the cashier: "I'm having a little last-minute get-together. Hope I have enough stuff! Hahaha." I'd laugh uncomfortably. "I know it's Tuesday, but I'm crazy like that!" Being bulimic is a little like being stoned; you're paranoid that everyone knows what you're up to and you have the munchies real bad.

Of course, I'd have to make the rounds to different stores, different nights of the week, for fear of running into the same cashiers. I practically needed a day runner to keep track. For a shortcut eating disorder, it certainly required a lot of planning.

Every day I'd tell myself that I wouldn't do it again, but then the smell of donuts or a commercial for Pizza Hut would come on and I'd feel my resolve start to crumble until eventually I'd end up facedown in a bowl of macaroni and cheese.

This seemingly unbreakable cycle continued until one evening, my roommate, who was supposed to be at her boyfriend's that night—as she was every night—made an impromptu visit to the apartment and flat out busted me.

She walked into the bathroom and found me retching into the toilet. I tried to tell her I was just drunk but it didn't take CSI to work this crime scene. The evidence was strewn all around my room: fast-food wrappers, empty ice cream containers . . . and I saw myself for what I'd become—it wasn't pretty.

Humiliated, I decided to try Overeaters Anonymous. In LA (and I'm sure everywhere else), there is a 12-step meeting for anything you can imagine being addicted to and a few things you'd never dream up: alcohol, food, cigarettes, shopping, narcotics, cocaine, gambling, sex, cluttering, and compulsive email checking come to mind, and that's just the tip of the iceberg.

I wasn't a complete stranger to these sorts of gatherings. I'd been to a few Alcoholic Anonymous meetings to support my friend "Tom," who was forced to go due to a court order. Tom got arrested after a long night of drinking in a club on Hollywood Boulevard. After closing time, he couldn't find his ride, so he wandered around in a drunken haze for a few hours, eventually climbing into an unlocked parked car and falling asleep only to be awakened by the police. I'm not sure why it was such a huge deal; it's not like he scored the nap at gunpoint, and he didn't even steal change out of the glove compartment. But the judge didn't see it that way and sentenced Tom to community service and three months of AA meetings.

The first time I went with him, a guy made a beeline for me as if I were a giant bottle of scotch with legs and extended a sweaty palm.

"Hi, my name is James. How long have you been sober?"

Is this a trick question? I wondered. "Well, I'm not," I said. "But I'm not *that* drunk. I could totally drive home right now. I'm just here to support my friend."

James gave me a condescending nod, threw a protective arm around my shoulder, and whispered conspiratorially, "You're in the right place." Before I could argue, he excused himself for a moment and came back with an *Are You an Alcoholic?* quiz—which I promptly failed. I'm sorry, but their criteria for what makes a person an alcoholic is very strict: *Have you suffered from blackouts?* Uh, not that I recall . . . *Have you ever had a drink in the morning?* Does a Bloody Mary count? Because everyone knows the only time it's acceptable to drink a Bloody Mary is around 7 a.m. So, if that counts, then *fine*, guilty. The point is, these people think everyone has a problem. If you say you only have a drink a night, they automatically assume you're distilling high-proof vodka out of potatoes in your bathtub.

Cultish nature aside, I loved listening to people lay bare the things they've done in life in the name of drinking. Being a person who will share with someone I just met in the ladies' room that I recently had an abortion and once tried to smoke heroin, I felt right at home. In AA they call this sharing; I call it dinner conversation. I listened intently to a man who looked like a kinder, jollier version of Santa Claus talk about accidentally killing his dog because he spent so much time drinking he forgot to feed it. I cried with a newcomer who said this was the first time he'd ever gone two days without drinking since he was nine years old. I threw a dollar in the donation basket and happily joined hands with Tom and a tatted-up teenager for the serenity prayer that ended with "Keep coming back! It works if you work it, so work it, you're worth it." I took in the looks on the alcoholics faces. Most of them looked downright serene. This was some good shit. It turned lives around!

But OA wasn't quite as fun.

First of all, in OA you don't get a cake for your one-year sobriety like in AA; just a candle. You'd think that after a year of not compulsively overeating they could at least throw a cupcake your way for your efforts. And being there for my own, very real problem wasn't nearly as entertaining. At least in AA they exchange war stories from their drinking days— more often than not there is prison involved. In OA, people talked about food—what they ate, what they didn't eat, what they thought about eating all day. It didn't give me hope; it just gave me ideas.

A few meetings in, a dark-haired mom type who looked about forty pounds overweight stood dejectedly in front of the room behind a podium and introduced herself as "Nancy, compulsive overeater." She confessed that she'd come *this* close—she held a sausage-size thumb and forefinger a millimeter apart—to overdosing on Valium after eating four boxes of Entenmann's Banana Crunch Cake the night before. The poor woman was so overwhelmed with the gravity of her confession; she collapsed into a pool of tears and self-loathing and had trouble continuing with her share. She stood there, hunched over, trying to catch her breath to go on when from the back of the room came an undignified knock on the table signifying Nancy's three minutes were over. A dozen hands shot up, desperate for their time in the spotlight.

A woman dressed in a short skirt with a blond ponytail perched high on top of her head, despite the fact that her cheerleader days clearly ended a good decade before, took the podium, smiling widely. Apparently, Nancy was already forgotten. I tried to submerge my inner cynic and listen.

"Hi, I'm Jeanne—anorexic."

"Hi, Jeanne," the crowd responded a little too enthusiastically—like human smiley face emoticons.

"Today was a healing day! I mean, for me, I can wake up and say 'Good morning, God' or 'Good God, it's morning' but I like to keep an attitude of gratitude!"

I couldn't help but think, for an anorexic, Jeanne had quite the muffin top going on—but, hey, I guess that's progress. She then droned on about either a commercial audition or talking lobsters . . . I couldn't tell you because poor Nancy was still crying so hard I worried she might hyperventilate in the corner. Of course, no one had a paper lunch sack for her to breathe into; it was bad form to bring snacks to OA. I mentally put the woman on a suicide watch, but Jeanne didn't seem to notice.

I couldn't help but think, *Doesn't admitting you almost offed yourself warrant at least a nod in the suicidal person's general vicinity? Or at least an extra minute at the podium?* Jeanne continued on, engrossed in her own inspirational platitudes. "If you have one foot in yesterday and one in tomorrow you will pee all over today," which will no doubt be the title of Judge Judy's next book.

Clearly a big problem with the 12-step format, besides how everyone seems to communicate solely through annoying slogans, is that addicts are narcissists by nature. And the last thing a narcissist wants to do is sit around listening to other people talk about themselves.

After the meeting, I hesitantly approached Nancy and recommended my last therapist, Huggybear. I knew they'd probably be a match. If this chick didn't need a hug, I don't know who did.

Although I was not at all convinced that I belonged in OA, I forced myself to attend a few more meetings, sitting silently in the back of the room and watching. I had less than no interest in participating.

One day, in a particularly irritating meeting, a woman in her early sixties led the group. She shared her story of where she'd been, what she'd done, and who she was now. The story culminated in, "So there I was at my mother's house just after my father's funeral. I looked at a tray of cocktail weenies, one of my 'trigger foods,' and, just for a moment, I thought of how good it would taste, how much I wanted one. But I knew that one would be too many and a thousand wouldn't be enough. So I called my sponsor."

I flashed forward to myself in ten years, finding out I was dying of an extremely rare form of pancreatic cancer and sitting in this same room, beating myself up for having a regular Yoplait instead of a nonfat Yoplait when I should be out having sex with a dumb as fuck but gorgeous blackjack dealer in Vegas or tipping over an ice cream truck and eating everything that fell out, *anything* but bitching about food in this suffocating church basement with subpar coffee and people who spoke in emoticons. Suddenly, I felt like I had to get the hell out of there. I needed some air; I couldn't breathe. I practically knocked over my folding chair in my hurry to escape.

Once outside, I took a seat on the steps of the building. It was the absolute perfect time to light up a smoke. Unfortunately for me, cigarettes were one of the few habits I'd never picked up.

I sat there and I thought about my childhood, one I was pretty sure Lifetime movie executives would salivate over. Sure I had some demons, demons I'd need to contend with if I was ever to have a full, happy life that included marriage to someone I allowed to touch me. But I wasn't like *these* people. I was *nothing* like these people, was I? Sure I related to *some* things, like when a woman said "no one has ever gone to 7-Eleven at midnight for broccoli" or that whole "one is too many and a thousand isn't enough" . . . shit . . . I sat there for a while and finally went back inside.

I raised my hand. "I'm Stefanie, bulimic."

"Hi, Stefanie" came the answer from the crowd of people so unlike me and so exactly like me.

My story came pouring out, well, three minutes of it. And I kept coming back. 'Cause, as I found out, it does work if you work it. But I refused to buy any "One Day at a Time" bumper stickers, and at the end of the year I had myself a fucking cupcake.

Fired Up!

During my early teens through my late twenties, I was fired from approximately thirty jobs, most of them waitressing. And that's not including the ones I kinda sorta left on my own sometimes kinda sorta in the middle of a shift.

It's surprising I would even wait tables to begin with, but, besides the cash tips and lack of early rousing required, waitressing jobs are easy to get and, not having gone to college, I didn't feel qualified to do much else. No one at a restaurant demands a master's degree in carrying hot plates or even extensive knowledge of how to work a cash register—most of them don't bother to ask for a reference, which is good because I left a job on good terms about as often as a gas station bathroom gets a thorough disinfecting.

Very possibly I would've continued on the path to becoming an only slightly less annoying version of Linda Lavin on *Alice* if I hadn't managed to get myself eighty-sixed from four jobs in the space of a month.

In LA, restaurants are like acting jobs—if you get fired from that many jobs, you are bound to become blacklisted. It's a small town and people talk. I was quickly becoming the Sean Young of the food service industry.

I'd been working in a Brazilian restaurant for just over six months, which was my own personal Guinness record. But, due to my outspoken nature and the South American owner's dislike of women with working vocal cords, I'd been skating on thin ice for almost as long as I'd had the job. I'd often come out with over-the-top suggestions like, "It's almost closing time. Maybe we should cut a server since there are six of us still on and only two tables." Or a doozy like, "Since we're out of grilled salmon, should we erase it from the 'specials board'?" I don't want to be too hard on myself though, since some of my suggestions were down-right helpful and selfless. Like the time I said to a customer who called me clueless, "Sorry, I was distracted by your hair plugs. Next time you might want to go all the way to the back." It's shocking I was never voted Employee of the Month.

Customer service is not my forte. I'm not really a people person, nor am I a "team player," and also, I *seem* to have a problem with authority. My personality type is wrong for a job where it's not acceptable to haul off and punch someone when he asks, "Is there dairy in this bleu cheese dressing?" Although, I'm not quite sure if there is a job where that would be acceptable, except maybe as a bouncer or cage fighter.

It wouldn't take Freud to figure out that this was probably a learned personality trait, considering that my stepfather's worldview seemed to scream "stick it to the man!" My stepfather reveled in taking unsuspecting people he'd felt had wronged him to small claims court like it was his job. Not to mention my mother's first husband, my father, was a comedian who never left his apartment without a pin on the brim of his hat that read, "Go Pound Sand Up Your Ass."

So, if you figure the acorn doesn't fall far from its family of origin, it would make sense that I've always had what teachers and bosses termed an "attitude problem."

Every day I'd drag myself in to work, waltz in with my Coffee Bean coffee, and try harder to get along. My last day on the job was no different.

"You're late," the manager, Robert, alerted me as I was punching in. I felt my resolve going down the shitter immediately. I never liked Robert. Besides the fact that pretty much anyone who purposely goes into restaurant management tends to have the diplomacy skills of Pol Pot and a cocaine habit that would rival Andy Dick's, Robert insisted that people pronounce his name Roh-bear-t. And he wasn't even from Brazil. He was from Ohio. I guess he was just entranced by the South American vibe of the place. I was also opposed to his soul patch—a popular look from the nineties I'd never understood. It seemed big with guys who think they're too cool for a goatee but don't want to give up entirely on the whole idea of chin pubes. Oh, and he always had bits of cilantro in his teeth.

"I'm actually exactly on time," I said, nonchalantly tossing my purse under the counter and grabbing a book of checks.

"No, you need to be here fifteen minutes prior to your shift. It's a courtesy. We've been through this."

"Well, if I have to be here fifteen minutes early, then it's not a courtesy and I should get paid for that fifteen minutes." I marched off to marry ketchups and give myself a little pep talk. For some reason, I talk to myself in lists:

1. Tone the complaining down a notch! You need this job.
2. No whining about the music even though The Gypsy Kings have been on an endless loop for three months.
3. Do not argue with any customers even if they are known bad tippers.
4. Restrain from writing "tip is not included!" on the customer's check in red marker.
5. Try harder not to sound like a hostage speaking to police while your captor stands over you with a knife when asking customers, "Would you care for a delicious spinach and cheese empanada to start your meal?"
6. Just for today you will not attempt to dissuade anyone from ordering the sweetbreads by explaining that . . . "Ewww . . . they're pancreas!"

A couple of hours into my shift, I flirtatiously topped off the wineglass of a regular customer, who was seated at the bar. He was pretty cute and I felt the gesture really smacked of good customer service. But Roh-bear-t, who was almost as opposed to attractive men as he was to flossing, apparently saw me pour the extra wine and a few minutes later pulled me aside.

"You gave that customer a glass of wine. I just looked; it's not on the check. You need to go back and add it in, otherwise you're going to pay for it."

I was outraged. I mean, it was hardly a *glass* of wine—more like the amount you would get in a rinsing cup at the dentist—and the guy was cute but upon further inspection more in a Judge Reinhold-y way than a throw-him-down-and-do-him-on-the-Spanish-tile type of way. I wasn't buying him a drink, but I also wasn't going to charge the poor guy for a full glass of wine.

The situation was actually ironic seeing as how I'd snuck a few bottles of Chilean Merlot home after a particularly stressful shift to be consumed later in my apartment. Really I owed the restaurant more than the price of a glass of wine, but I was standing on principle, dammit!

I refused. Roh-bear-t was practically beaming as he said the words I'd heard many times before. "Turn in your apron and go home."

If I had even the slightest amount of impulse control or a sneak peek at the cable bill waiting for me, I might've apologized and asked for another chance, but instead I put my apron on the counter and walked out.

I always imagined this day to end with me going out Tarantino-style: sliding open the glass dessert case and in one fell swoop smashing every last plate of flan to the floor, leaving the dulce de leche sauce oozing into the cracks of the tile floor like blood; then I'd kick in the Panasonic stereo and drag its carcass out into the middle of the floor where I'd stomp on it until "Bamboleo" skipped for all of eternity. I'd end my rampage by showering the whole place with machine-gun fire and then popping sixteen Qualuudes (provided they're still manufactured).

Unfortunately, until I got a few more paychecks, I wouldn't be able to afford bail, let alone illicit street drugs, so instead I walked out onto the promenade into a sea of happy tourists and cried angry, embarrassed tears all the way back to my car.

I spent a couple of afternoons licking my wounds and watching my now basic cable where the advertising is aimed at out-of-work losers like me. I contemplated a whole new career entering the exciting world of calligraphy or experiencing the freedom of the road as a Long Haul truck driver—who knew I could train for either job in just six short weeks? I'd also answered a can-you-draw-this? ad in a magazine and although I hadn't heard back yet, I felt fairly confident that I had a full scholarship to art school in my back pocket. But in the end, I took the path of least resistance and decided to go back to waiting tables.

It's not like I hadn't tried other jobs in customer service. I was great in the interview. Most interviewers aren't all that creative, so it's a good bet that they will fall back on that same question, "What are your strengths and weaknesses?" I just made sure I was prepared. The key is not to give any real weakness; no one wants to hear, "Well, I'm not a stickler for honesty" or "I'm rarely on time." Instead I'd say, "I can drive people a bit crazy with my perfectionism" or "I'm way too obsessive when it comes to getting a job done right!" with a conspiratorial smile as if to say, "All this selflessness is such a thorn in my side but what are you gonna do?" But although I could get the job, I lacked follow-through—like the time I got let go from a job at a movie theater for refusing to wear white shoes. It wasn't so much an outright *refusal* to wear white shoes, just that I didn't own any. Besides nurses and Wayne Newton, who wears *white* shoes? On the beginning of my third day at work, I was called out on my black Doc Martens by my boss, Bob.

"Where are your white shoes? It's a requirement of this job that you wear white shoes. I can't let you work past Friday if you don't have the proper footwear."

"Sorry, I forgot to buy them again." My reasoning for not making the white shoes my number one priority was that I was *standing behind the concession stand the whole time;* no one would be seeing my feet anyway, so what difference did it make? I could've been wearing orange shoes, clown shoes, or eight-inch stiletto heels for all it mattered. Weirdly, Bob didn't see it that way.

Seeking the easiest and quickest way to restore my cable, I sucked it up and took the next available waitressing job I could find. The pickings were getting slimmer; this time it was a sports bar. The owner, a doughy-looking frat-boy type, hired me on the spot under the condition that I wear sexy athletic shorts. With visions of HBO getting turned back on, I reluctantly agreed. This was pretty radical of me because first of all, I'm a hard-core feminist and second of all, I have fat knees and make it a strict practice to avoid allowing them out in public.

The frat boy turned out to be quite the douche bag. Have you ever met a frat boy who wasn't? But this guy's sadistic streak went way beyond a little innocent frat-house date rape. My first night there, he fired a female bartender with stage four ovarian cancer and no health insurance because he thought she was "too slow." I was mortified. Did he think that chemo was like a shot of ginseng?

Within a few days, he drunk dialed me at 4 a.m. to ask whether I'd gotten home okay and to see if he could "stop by." I meant to say a simple no but what came out was, "Are you fucking kidding me?"

The very next evening, while toting a plate of potato skins stuffed with sour cream and Bac-O-Bits to a four top, I was pulled into the office by the assistant manager and fired for "not having a friendly attitude," which was true but sort of beside the point in this situation.

Out of work again, I was nervous. The obvious next step would be suing the pants off of Frat Boy for sexual harass-ment, but I knew from watching *Erin Brockovich* back when I had HBO that a landmark case like this could drag on for years in the court system before it snakes its way to the Supreme Court and I needed to pay my rent within the week.

So the next day at the crack of 3 p.m., I hoofed my way farther up the same street.

A few blocks north, I found an Irish bar I'd actually frequented a few times. I seemed sort of Irish that day anyway with my hair in braids, a Greek fisherman's cap on my head, and drunk off of the three Sam Adams I downed to dull the pain of job hunting. I thought I was pretty cute, and if you're of the mind-set that looking like a poor man's Punky Brewster is adorable and appropriate for a woman in her late-twenties, you might have agreed.

I must've had the luck of the Irish on my side because they'd just lost a waitress and needed someone to start that very night. I was so relieved, I went home and had another celebratory beer!

When I returned a few hours later with a fairly bad headache, the place was a ghost town. No owner, no other waitress to show me the ropes, and a bartender who looked like a homeless version of Colin Farrell smoking an American Spirit behind the bar. I briefly wondered if he had a girlfriend and if not, whether making out with him in the stockroom might help pass the time, but his brogue was so strong he was useless to me.

Suddenly at nine o'clock on the dot, the entire population of Dublin showed up all at once. So with no instruction, I had no choice but to start taking orders. By 10 p.m. the bar was in full manic drunken swing and I'd already had my ass pinched twice. I hadn't heard of men actually pinching a woman's ass since *The Benny Hill Show* was considered high entertainment and I felt humiliated. I stood outside of myself and really took stock of my situation. *I am twenty-six years old (fine, twenty-eight)! There has to be something else I could do for a living.*

I tried to think through my other options: Although I had the requisite low self-esteem and daddy issues, I had way too much cellulite to be a stripper; I loved to argue but since I'd barely graduated high school, high-paid attorney was probably not in my immediate future. I briefly considered having a baby just to get a little state funding.

A sloppy drunk woman in black-and-white-striped Spandex pants, which on her thighs looked less like stripes and more like lightning bolts, yanked at the back of my tank top, pulling me out of my mental soul search, and slurred, "I need you to fetch a round of drinks for my group ponto." *Ponto.* She was so drunk she'd lost the use of the letter r. When I returned with the drinks, she screamed over the blaring Sinead O' Connor song, "Nother round!" I might have done her bidding despite all the finger snapping, which, as a waitress, was my least favorite mode of communication, but she didn't even tip me for the first round. I decided to "forget" her next round of drinks. And the one after that. And the one after that, until she complained to *her friend* the bartender.

"Lass, I'm afraid we're gonna have to let you go." Because of his brogue there was a very slight chance he said, "Would you like to go see Bono?" but it was doubtful. I tried hard not to show any emotion, pretending it was the smoke from his fifteenth American Spirit causing my eyes to tear; after all, I'd been here, in this predicament, a million times. Why was this time any different?

I slunk out the back door, looking both ways to make sure that the drunk woman and her pants weren't lying in wait in the parking lot. No one was there but my Buick Skyhawk. I turned the motor over and the interior of the car was illuminated by the empty gas tank light.

Fired in one night. Was it me? Would someone else have put up with that crap? It didn't seem like my situation could get any worse. But then it did.

The next day, a friend set me up on an interview at the restaurant where she worked. I knew this restaurant to be very corporate—surely there would be a name tag involved and a very long list of flavored martinis to memorize, not to mention a two-week training period much like boot camp where I would be quizzed endlessly on how to put the modifier for cheddar cheese into the computer, but I was running out of options.

The very next afternoon I found myself seated in a booth across from the manager, a man in a dark Men's Wearhouse suit and tie, shiny black dress shoes, and a pencil-thin mustache that I couldn't stop staring at. The man, who introduced himself as Bob, was staring at me intently, too.

"You look very familiar," he said, in what I perceived as a slightly accusatory tone.

"I get that a lot. I've got one of those faces." I tried not to sound paranoid. He looked ever so slightly familiar, too, but

I couldn't place him. I was, like, ninety-five percent sure I'd never slept with him.

"Did you ever work at a movie theater?" Bob asked, not unlike someone administering a lie detector test.

"Well . . . once, a while ago, but not for very long. Waitressing is really what I love to do." If I *had* been hooked up to a lie detector, I imagined the needle would be leaving jagged marks up and down the page.

"Pacific West Theaters. You refused to buy white shoes. I fired you."

I was so shocked, I actually peed in my pants a little bit. Something I hadn't done since I'd been busted for shoplifting penny candy at Woolworth's when I was seven.

"Oh, you're *that* Bob. Hi, again," was all I could think of to say.

Once I got myself home and changed my underwear, I realized I felt relieved in a way. I knew my career in customer service had finally come full circle. Something had to change—and that something was going to have to be me. I had to get it together—get a "new attitude," like Patti LaBelle, but maybe not quite as positive—I had my limitations.

I purchased a used copy of *What Color Is Your Parachute?*, which I perused over my last "borrowed" bottle of Chilean wine, scanning chapters and making a list of my personality traits to find my perfect career:

- Good at bullshitting
- Few real job skills

- Strong dislike of being told what to do
- Bossy
- Loud
- Lots of ideas but not a lot of follow-through
- Tendency to drink too much in social situations

I don't know if it was the alcohol, the spirit of Patti LaBelle, or the book had magic powers, but suddenly the world opened up to me. It turned out there *were* jobs perfect for people with what I had to offer. I could be a politician, Shannen Doherty, or even a Hollywood producer, which ended up being my true calling. And it only took me thirty-four jobs to get there.

Gimme Shelter

The month I turned sixteen I found myself the best-dressed girl at a runaway shelter. That summer was not a good one. You know those After School Specials where a mom with a very young daughter gets divorced and then quickly remarries her ex-husband's best friend—who just happens to have some anger-management issues? And then the girl, most likely played by Kristy McNichol, grows up feeling she's never able to do right by her stepfather, who is likely to explode over being asked to turn up the heat in the car or punch a wall over a request to please pass the butter? Of course, the mom (most likely played by Patty Duke) refuses to believe a single negative thing about her husband and goes on to have more kids with him. Over the years, Kristy McNichol's character predictably becomes angry and withdrawn—the black sheep of the family. She starts to drink, skips school to hang out at McDonald's, constantly gets into trouble with the assistant vice principal, Mr. Ward, for forging absentee excuses, gets caught, and eventually is on the outs with everyone in her family. Let's just say if there was an After School Special like this I would have *completely* related.

Between my sophomore and junior years of high school, my parents, restless from living in a small city with a lack of diversity, decided to move across the country to a similarly sized city with even less diversity. Since they had nowhere to stay while they looked for a house, my parents were thrilled to be offered a temporary place to crash with their friend Connie-Sue and her preteen daughter. Being relocated three thousand miles from my best friend, my high school, and my comfort zone only ratcheted up the long-brewing tensions in my family. By the time we were settled into our temporary digs, profanity-filled fights with my stepfather in front of everyone were a daily occurrence. Looking back, it must've seemed shocking to Connie-Sue's daughter to hear words like "cocksucker" flying around her living room, especially coming from a teenage girl. After so many years of threats, I'd stopped caring about the consequences of fighting back. I'd stopped caring about much.

The combination of moving, preparing to start a new job, and dealing with the constant battles between husband and daughter while trying to keep from getting kicked out of Connie-Sue's proved too much for my mother, and she lost it during a particularly draining argument. My mother felt forced to make a choice, and I wasn't it. My mother screamed for me to get out and never come back.

As far back as I could remember, when given a choice, my mother had not chosen me. But she was my mother and, although the whole situation was shitty and I didn't understand it, I loved her. She was all I had and I chose to believe, I *had* to believe, that she'd see she was making a horrible mistake. I had to believe she loved me.

At first, I tried to think of being on my own as an adventure, dramatic, and a bit glamorous. I snuck back into the house, rummaged through Connie-Sue's kitchen, and gathered as many granola snack bags as I could find—which was only three—a few packages of string cheese, and a thermos of water (I didn't want to dehydrate—I'd heard somewhere that the first thing that kills you is the dehydration). Then I set out for parts unknown. I was like Christopher Columbus out to discover Springfield, Massachusetts. It took about twelve blocks and thirty minutes for the glamour to wear off, the food to run out, and the anxiety to set in. I sat down on someone's front lawn to go over my options while trying not to panic.

My parents couldn't be serious, could they? Would they actually think that I could survive on my own in a city I'd lived in approximately four days? I was like a domesticated cat; as much as I put up a surly front, I still longed for affection and a warm place to curl up. Plus, I really enjoyed seafood.

Maybe I could just go back to Connie-Sue's, I thought. Maybe, possibly, my mother wasn't serious. But I knew she was. I tried to think sensibly about my options. I could go to the police but what would I tell them? My mom kicked me out so you need to go talk to her and tell her to let me back in? That didn't really seem like a workable idea. Plus, I was embarrassed that my parents didn't want me and wasn't excited to advertise it to the city's police department.

Instead, I made my way about a mile away to the grocery store pay phone and made a mental list of people to call (collect). It was a very short list. My aunt Lucy lived in New Jersey and I'd been at her house for a few days before I arrived in Springfield. She'd also once taken me for an entire summer when I was nine, and although she'd forced me to take flute lessons, I'd had a pretty good time. Surely she'd send me a bus ticket. I called her and when she answered right away, relief flooded my system.

"Aunt Lucy!" I felt the tears burning my eyes immediately the way you always do when you're hurt and although you try to stay strong as soon as you hear your mom's voice you break down. But I tried to keep it together—I knew she didn't need a basket case on her hands. "Aunt Lucy, Mom kicked me out of the house and I have nowhere to go. *Please* can I come stay with you? She says I can never come back. She says I'm no longer her daughter. I don't know what to do."

"Stefanie, you have to calm down. There is no way that your mom would just leave you out in the street. Just call her and talk to her. I'm absolutely positive that this is a misunderstanding. But I can't get into the middle of it. Call her. It'll work out." And with that sage advice, she hung up.

I briefly entertained the idea of calling my biological

father in Los Angeles, but I knew he was newly on his fourth marriage to a woman in her early twenties and they'd just had a baby. It just wasn't an option. There was no one else to call. Like I said, it was a short list. I sat down on the curb in front of the pay phone and sobbed. This wasn't supposed to happen to people like me; people who wore clothes from *Fred Segal*, dammit. I didn't look homeless. I probably looked like any kid in any town on her way home from summer camp or singing lessons, but I felt like the Russian nesting dolls my mother collected. Every time something happened, another outer protective layer was taken off and I was left a little smaller than before. I just hoped that things would turn around before there was nothing left.

All of a sudden, like in a movie, a Volkswagen bug pulled into the parking lot and out of a city of strangers, I saw a face I recognized. It was the lifeguard from the Jewish Community Center pool where I'd been dropped off while my parents unloaded the car, earlier in the week. The girl hopped out of the passenger door and came to my side. Thank God Jews love nothing more than to get involved with other people's problems. When she found out what was going on, she went right into busybody mode. "Okay, I know a girl whose parents are out of town for the night. She lives pretty close by, and I'm sure she'd let you stay with her and then tomorrow we can figure something else out."

I was in no position to say no. So off to a complete stranger's house I went. The girl was kind enough to make me a little dinner and let me sleep on her couch. Although humiliated, I must say the frozen pizza was delicious. Shame has never really put a damper on my taste buds. But the next day, the girl told me I'd have to go because her dad was coming home. I really couldn't understand why I couldn't just move in with her. They had a huge house in a nice section of town, which was a lesson I took with me. When I later moved out to California and didn't have a place to stay one night, I slept in my car. But not before driving to Beverly Hills and parking in front of the most expensive house I could find. Much like *having* a home, being homeless is all about location.

I was completely out of ideas. So, after wandering around most of the day, I called my mother. To say she wasn't excited to hear from me would be a gross understatement. But, to my great relief, she didn't sound surprised, either. For some ridiculous reason, I half expected her to say something like, "Thank God you're all right. I made a huge mistake and I want you to come home right now. We can work this out. I love you, Sweetie." What I didn't expect was what she did say: "You are not welcome to stay here. But I have found a shelter where you can go. They can't take you in until tomorrow, so for tonight you can sleep in the car and I'll drive you there in the morning."

I walked back the few miles to Connie-Sue's. Without entering her house, I climbed into the back of our gray Jeep Wagoneer and fell asleep in the doggy odor that permeated the vinyl seats from our springer spaniel, Louie, and our Alaskan malamute, Conan—the smell still clinging to my clothes in the morning.

When I arrived at the shelter, I was an odd sight. Apparently it's not the norm for parents to pull up and drop their kid off like the shelter is some sort of day care for teens and not a crisis center for kids scooped off the streets. No wonder I got the evil stare from the group of runaways, which could just as easily been the touring company of *Oliver* or *Annie.* It didn't help my cause that I was wearing a spiffy new red mini-skirt and matching blouse with a sailor's knot at the neck, a present from my biological father's wife. I must've looked like a slightly more ethnic Shirley Temple with a major chip on her shoulder. The way people were looking at me, I'm sure they thought I was about to break into a rendition of "Good Ship Lollipop" and blow everyone kisses before my sign-in was complete. God, I hoped they had MTV. I had a bad feeling I wasn't going to be making friends.

Once my mother drove off, I was shown to my room by the director of the program, a kind, obese black woman named Gladys. I was led through the family room, where a couple of boys, Chris and Jeremy, were sitting around playing cards and reading comic books. Chris looked up and gave me a "hey." And Jeremy, with long, dark, stringy hair and an earring, didn't even look up. I immediately considered him a person of interest.

We had to walk up a short flight of stairs to get to the bedrooms, and Gladys seemed out of breath by the time we made it up to the top. I had a twin bed with a musty, faded bedspread and a lumpy pillow that looked like it was made out of some kind of cheap foam padding. On the other twin bed in the room sat my new roommate.

"This is Tammy. You'll be sharing a room with her. Get settled in and then come downstairs, and in the meantime, I'll get you set up on the chores sheet." *Chores sheet?* Wow, things just kept getting better. While I put the blanket and pillowcase on my bed which had been left folded on top, Tammy introduced herself.

"I'm a prostitute," she said as casually as if she was telling me her astrological sign.

"Oh?" I tried not to look shocked. The girl couldn't have been older than fourteen. She wasn't even wearing fishnets— just no-label jeans and an old ratty sweatshirt that looked like she may have found it in the trash. Prostitution seemed so out of my realm. I tried to figure out how to respond, but it turned out a response wasn't necessary. This one was a talker.

"My boyfriend, Zeke, was my pimp, but I couldn't stand it anymore so I took off and now he's coming after me. He's threatened to bomb the place. He totally wants me dead. I don't have pass privileges because he may be waiting outside. So if you go to the store, can you get me some BBQ chips and a Kit Kat bar? I could totally use a sugar fix." While she talked, she poked through my belongings and stopped suddenly, holding up a periwinkle angora sweater with flared sleeves. "Fuck me running! Where you get this? It's wicked gorgeous!"

"My grandmother bought it for me at Macy's when I went to visit her in New York."

I hadn't shared a room with anyone in years, especially

a prostitute on the run from her pimp. It made me nervous, but I tried to be cool. "My mom's a bitch. And my stepfather hates me."

"Really?" Tammy perked up. "My mother's asshole boyfriend raped me so I took off. Stole his dog, too. But Zeke has him now." Jesus. It wasn't a "whose life sucks worse?" competition, yet I was already feeling like a fraud. On the other hand, I was here, so somewhere things had veered way off track for both of us.

I had to pee, so Tammy showed me to the bathroom we'd be sharing. On the sink was a huge can of Aqua Net, a clear Ziploc bag full of drugstore makeup, and about nine bottles of prescription medication lining a shelf.

"I'm manic-depressive," she said, gesturing to the bottles.

"Oh, yeah? My biological father has that, too," I said, trying to bond.

"I hear it's genetic. Anyway, let's go eat," Tammy said. "Breakfast is at 7 a.m. sharp and then there's cleanup and chores, but it's almost ten so we can have a snack." Tammy seemed hyperfocused on food, which meant either she was a woman after my own heart or this place was really fucking boring.

"Great."

According to the chore sheet I found in the kitchen, I had toilet scrubbing, dinner dishes, dusting, and vacuuming to look forward to on my first day. Everything was on a level system and since I was new, I was a level one, which I quickly found out carried very few—ok, no—privileges with it. I had to earn the right to have dessert, watch television, walk to the store, go to bed later than 9 p.m., and even use the phone. This whole system seemed entirely unfair. This wasn't a juvenile detention center; these kids were in need of someone who cared about them. They weren't here because they'd committed crimes. I had been dropped off by my parents not because I was into drugs or alcohol or shoplifting but because I was argumentative. The rules and strictness seemed oppressive and worse than boot camp. Before we moved, I'd considered trying to join the military, but it didn't seem doable, mainly because I was too young and I doubted they would take someone with a physical impairment like contact lenses, so I had ruled it out.

My first night, I went to my room straight after dinner and read *If There Be Thorns,* the latest in my favorite V. C. Andrews series, until Tammy came in looking distraught and shaky. She said she was certain she'd heard her boyfriend sneaking around outside, and although she didn't see him, she knew he was there. We sat and listened for a long time, but I never heard anything and eventually fell asleep.

By day three, no one had heard from my mother. The hope that she'd have regretted her decision and come right back to get me had faded, and I was becoming accustomed to the routine. Other than Tammy, I hadn't really talked to many kids. But I'd been given store privileges and spent some of the five dollars I had on a pack of Hostess Snowballs, which I snuck and ate during "group." These days the pros would call it therapy, but at the time it was more of a rap session.

If it was possible to have a favorite part of the day, group was it. People were encouraged to address why they were here during the session, which was run by a resident counselor who'd for three straight days worn the same dingy jeans and gray fisherman's wool sweater. I started to suspect that this was his uniform to make the kids feel like he was just like them. I found this vaguely comforting, along with his habit of never being able to get his glasses to sit straight on his nose in spite of endless adjustments. The best thing about him was his laid-back demeanor. He never pressured anyone to talk, but if you did he listened as if there could be a pop quiz. Plus, he smoked cigarettes compulsively—about a pack an hour—which seemed to somehow draw out even the toughest, moodiest among us. Maybe his compulsive side made him more human, more relatable, or maybe the steady secondhand nicotine just eased the anxiety. Most of the kids staying there were pretty sad cases: unwanted, molested, wards of the court, bounced from foster home to foster home with the shelter serving as a holding cage between nightmarish situations. I suppose it made me feel better about my life when I compared myself with them.

Jeremy, the guy I'd noticed on the first day, turned out to be fifteen and on the run from his fourth abusive foster home. Another kid was there because his father had recently been arrested as a suspected serial killer. This sort of put things with my stepfather in perspective. I considered recategorizing him as "menacing but manageable."

I definitely was falling for Jeremy, mainly because he thus

far hadn't showed the least bit of interest in my existence—a highly attractive quality in a potential mate considering the strongest feelings I'd harbored for a boy to that point had been Matt Dillon. I watched Jeremy out of the corner of my eye and tried to imagine what he smelled like and what it would be like to run my fingers through his hair. At closer inspection, the ratted tangles made me realize I'd definitely need to brush it first, but somehow that only added to the intrigue.

I popped a little foamy marshmallow with coconut coating into my mouth and—possibly due to the sugar high— began feeling some hope. Just two more years and I could legally work and get the hell out of this city. Maybe I'd move to Los Angeles. Maybe I'd go find my dad. Maybe I'd be an actress and become famous so everyone would know I was somebody—somebody worthwhile. Maybe my mother would see then. Maybe she'd know what she was missing.

Around day five, dressed in a flawlessly broken-in pair of Levi 501's and a purple-and-gray-striped Izod sweater, I called a meeting in the room I still shared with Tammy. "Listen, guys. I think it's bullshit that we get to watch only an hour of TV a day even if we're at level three. I can live with some of the other rules, but I feel it's our God-given right to watch television and we should fight for it." The other kids looked at me intently, if a bit suspiciously. Most of them were certainly up for a good fight. They just needed a ringleader, and this was my specialty—a way to get in with the group and get them to at last see past my embarrassing possession of two married middle-class Jewish parents.

"I'm ready to start a petition," I chirped. I'd been listening to Pat Benatar's "Hell Is for Children" over and over on my Walkman and I was pretty riled up.

"I've been back here ten times and nothing ever changes here except the staff," said a boy who'd I'd never heard speak out loud before. I chose to take him talking at all as encouraging.

"Look, if enough of us argue for it, we can make them see things our way. But we should start small. Let's just ask for two hours of TV a day."

"And that people on every level should be allowed dessert," Tammy piped in, voicing her pro-sugar platform. "We're not in jail." The truth of the matter was I'd been holed up in Connie-Sue's basement watching hours of MTV every day and was in serious withdrawal. I would've traded my later bedtime privilege for even half a J. Geils or Bananarama video. I was that desperate. But the shelter didn't have cable, which was another thing I wanted to add to the petition. Cable TV was a necessity as far as I was concerned. Really, at that point, I was dying to tune out—as we all were. Some had found other ways to do it.

The shelter was strict, but pot was abundant. I was offered a chance to "smoke out" with at least half the kids, including Tammy, whom I wasn't entirely sure should be mixing marijuana with her mood-stabilizing meds. I passed on the pot: I found being stoned the opposite of relaxing. Unless I was by myself, surrounded by food and in no danger of any social interaction, I was okay, but that was rare.

So instead, I threw myself into reworking the shelter privilege system. I wrote up a petition outlining the reasons we should be allowed to watch two hours of television as opposed to one. With Tammy's help, I went around to each resident and asked for a signature. I even camped outside the bathroom to wait for Greg, a brand-new arrival, to come out of the shower. I meant business, and if that entailed seeing a little "accidental" nudity I wouldn't let that stand in my way. Last up was Jeremy. He took the paper out of my hand, signed it, handed it back, and looked me in the eye before shutting his door. He may as well have asked me to the prom. Things almost couldn't have gotten any better when Tammy yelled, *"Dinner!"*

I'd been in the shelter a little over a week when I went to Gladys's office to present my petition. She seemed out of breath and a touch sweaty despite the fact that she was just sitting at her desk doing paperwork.

"Gladys, some of the other kids and I feel that we should be allowed a few more privileges. I understand that you have to have rules around here and make things fair, but it really feels like we're being punished. Maybe just some extra TV would go a long way to making kids feel more at home. So, um, we signed a petition."

"You can't fight the system, honey." Then, without warning, she sprang the news on me that I was leaving. Most runaways could only stay for two weeks max and the main problem for me, and apparently the state of Massachusetts, was that I didn't run away. There wasn't enough funding to keep a kid in the system who had other viable options. My parents had been called and alerted to this fact. My mother had reluctantly agreed to pick me up the following morning. Gladys asked me how I felt about it—the eighties were a time big on feelings.

"I don't know," I told her honestly.

"Is there anything I should know when I make my report?" I looked down at my fingernails. As a chronic nail biter, my ragged cuticles were often bleeding and the whole look was something of an eyesore. But I noticed they were actually starting to grow a little. Maybe in a few weeks I could actually paint them.

"About your home life?" Gladys pushed.

"I don't know." Again, I really didn't know. I'd long since given up hope that anyone could really help me. But, my spirit wasn't broken, maybe just badly bruised. Deep inside I didn't believe I was such a bad kid. Somewhere buried beneath the self-centered, stupid, ugly, difficult, contrary label I'd been given was a very small voice—so small I had to be very, very quiet and calm to hear it—that voice said gently, "You'll be okay." That's all. The voice couldn't tell me what I'd do for a living or if I'd ever find a husband or have a house or children. The voice just told me I'd get through the next few minutes, the next month, the next year. What I did know was this past week had contained the least drama I'd experienced in a long time. To call it peaceful might be stretching it, but it was close. And shit, I'd managed to work myself to a level three in my short time there, I could go to bed at eleven if I felt like it, and I sort of had a boyfriend.

"No, I guess not."

"Well, then pack your things. Your mother is coming for you in the morning. And I'll think about the television, Stefanie. But don't get those kids' hopes up."

Driving away from the shelter with my mother the next day, we didn't speak. It was then that I knew I'd lost her. During the week I'd been gone, she and my stepfather had bought a house, and we were on our way there now. In the fall I'd be starting at a new high school. I'd be in my junior year. I thought about the kids I'd just driven away from. Were they starting school, too? Would any of them be at my new school? My mother put the radio on to a talk station and stared straight ahead, navigating her way to our new place while I stared out the window watching completely unfamiliar surroundings buzz by at thirty-five miles per hour. I thought about Tammy and smiled to myself. I knew she'd love my periwinkle sweater that I'd left behind for her on her bed. But I knew she'd enjoy the four Kit Kat bars I'd wrapped inside the sweater even more.

Reaching for the Stars

E very comedian dreams of landing his or her first shot at performing on television, and I was no exception—so it was a highly pressurized night at the Improv comedy club in Hollywood the evening of the *Star Search* auditions. About seventeen of us comics—all at different levels of experience— had made it onto a list to audition for the producers of the show, and most of us were completely freaking out—even the pros—but especially me. I was cursing myself because I'd accidentally taken some cold medicine earlier in the day to combat a lingering sinus headache, and I was still dealing with the ugly aftermath of a bad pseudoephedrine high.

The two glasses of wine I'd already downed at the bar weren't taking a bite out of my nerves, and standing in the hallway with the other comedians wasn't helping, either. A Jerry Seinfeld look-alike was cursing to anyone who would listen about the comic currently onstage.

"That asshole just did my joke. He knows I do that bit! Now I can't do it. It's my *opener!*" I knew that any comic listening to him would be secretly pleased. It's a competitive business and another's misfortune only gives the rest of us a better chance. Annoyingly, at least three comics were "warming up" before their set. I've never really gotten the whole Rocky Balboa shadow boxing or deep knee bend before a performance. It's not an athletic event. Looking at them, I couldn't help but think that as comedians, we're standing onstage in front of a microphone talking. It's either going to be funny or not. Being extra limber doesn't seem like it's going to make any difference. But, I wasn't going to dare tell that to the impressionist standing by the men's room doing lunges—comics take their comedy very, very seriously.

I'd been struggling doing stand-up for at least four years already when I got this big chance. And dammit, I deserved it. I'd endured more than my share of humiliation performing in sports bars while people ate chili fries and watched a Lakers' game over my head, cheering not for my jokes but for Robert Horry's three-point buzzer-beating game winner; screaming out jokes at a county fair while standing on top of stacked speakers from the bad Fog Hat cover band who played before me; attempting to humor teens at a drug recovery center while they sat twitching and detoxing from narcotics—and those were some of the better gigs. Any comedian who brags that he or she can work with any audience has simply not performed enough times in front of enough audiences. Try being the only Jewish female comedian at a born-again Christian "Bible Comedy Night." When my friend Lisa, a hilarious stand-up comic, gets asked, "Wow, stand-up sounds so hard. Do you ever bomb?" she always answers the same way. "Of course! Sometimes I'm super funny and sometimes the audience sucks."

By ceaselessly doing any stand-up gig I could to practice, I'd eventually worked my way into a few regular spots at the local bigger clubs and that eventually led to the *Star Search* showcase.

Out of the bunch of us auditioning, we all knew that only a couple of us would be chosen to fly to Orlando and get that highly coveted spot on what was at the time still a highly rated show.

Twenty minutes later, I'd just walked off the stage where I'd managed to get through my five minutes and had taken a seat at the bar, when a well-dressed man walked up to me and stuck out his hand. "I'm Sam Riddle from *Star Search* and I'd like to invite you to perform on our little show." I was speechless. Nothing that exciting had ever happened to me in my entire life. I was going to be on TV for the first time. And it wasn't even cable. It was network television, baby. Finally, my hard work had paid off—in spades! Now it was just a matter of time until I had my own sitcom. I wondered who they would get to play my mother or wacky neighbor and whether I would have any say in the casting process. I did have someone in mind for the role of the quirky best friend, although she was a little green, but I thought if she got into acting classes soon enough she could be ready. I wouldn't be

one of those people who forgot where she'd come from once
the big paychecks started rolling in. When I was rightfully
living in a gated community next door to people like Mariah
Carey, I'd still have the same friends, only now I'd be able to
get them work—even if that meant just being my driver. Of
course, being my driver would be a big responsibility and
would require a clean driving record. But there would also be
opportunities in merchandising and eventually the handling
of my clothing line. The more I thought about it, the more
I realized that my being famous was going to require a lot of
work and good managerial skills.

But right now the ticket to my success was standing right
in front of me waiting for a response.

"Thank you so much, Sam. I look forward to it."

This was big time, so my friends and I celebrated over
cocktails and three orders of deep-fried Buffalo wings. I
wouldn't be getting my own show for a few months, so I
figured I had plenty of time to hit the gym.

A few weeks later, I was flown to Orlando, Florida, where
the show was taped in front of a huge studio audience. My
flight wasn't "officially" first class, but I did get a window seat,
so the pampering had already begun. Plus, there was a driver
at the airport to personally take me to the Disney World hotel
where I'd be put up for the duration of my stay, which could
be long depending on how many shows I won. Let's just say,
I did not pack light.

Once I was settled into my hotel room, I got a call from
one of the producers to give me my schedule and go over my

jokes with me. I'd get only about three and a half minutes, so I needed to make that time count. I'd gone over and over my act—the act I'd pieced together with surgical precision—on the five-hour plane ride (nonstop!).

"Tonight you'll get taken to a local club to practice your set, if you like. The crowds in Orlando are incredible. Then tomorrow morning you'll be taken into the park to do a quick 'pretape bit,' and then tomorrow evening it's showtime. Any questions?" I wanted to ask, "Does the network that airs your sitcom hire someone to answer your fan mail, or is that something your personal staff has to deal with?" but I figured it could wait until after my first performance. Plus, my mouth was full of the mint I'd found on my pillow.

Later, at the local comedy club where I was to perform my act with the other comedians scheduled for shows that week, I found out I would be competing against a friend of mine, Keith, the following night on the big show. Keith went on a few acts before me and he killed—the audience couldn't get enough. Damn. I instantly felt bad. I mean, poor Keith deserved this chance as much as I did. He was an extremely funny guy, but besides that he was also a really nice person. And if this was a "nice person" competition, I wouldn't have stood a chance, but it was a talent competition so I really hoped Keith had a backup plan.

The next day was a flurry of activity. I went into the main park with some of the other contestants from my show for a couple of hours. I tried to befriend the reigning Female Vocalist champion, Angelina, but after securing a place in the semifinals she'd already begun acting like a diva and was out of touch with what the rest of us were going through.

"Were you nervous?" I asked her, trying to be friendly.

"Please. Have you heard me sing? The judges love me." When she said the word *love,* she dragged out the *o* like she was suddenly speaking Italian. "I got four stars for every performance." And with that she turned to her friend, the latest Spokesmodel winner, and ignored me.

"So, I take that to mean you don't get nervous," I said into thin air. And for the life of me I couldn't fathom how the Spokesmodel won, seeing as she had bigger teeth than Gary Busey's. I would have killed to see who her competition could've been.

"I get nervous," said a small voice behind me. It was an adorable nine-year-old, Yvette, who was competing in the Junior Vocalist category—finally a friend. The two of us immediately hit it off like gangbusters and sat together at the over-the-top catered lunch while we talked about how excited we were about the show, which parts, if any, of the Spokes-model hadn't been surgically altered, and of course, boys. The only problem was Yvette's mom had to hang out with us the whole day. She followed us around everywhere like some kind of obsessive stage mother. It was sort of embarrassing since she was old—like *my* age.

Before I knew it, I was having my makeup done back-stage, where I was offered coffee, tea, Red Vines, and finger sandwiches. To be honest, the last thing I wanted was coffee, but a beer would've been nice. If I'd known it was going to be a "dry" studio, I would've snuck one from the minibar in my hotel room. I also wanted my makeup toned down a bit since with the bright orange blush and overly smoky eye shadow I looked like I could've been auditioning for the part of a streetwalker in a Broadway musical or possibly a flushed raccoon. But when I brought it to the makeup lady's attention, she assured me it would look completely natural on camera.

From backstage, in my makeup chair, I was able to watch the show from a monitor while it was in progress. My category was coming up, and I was being ushered toward the stage by a person with a walkie-talkie while the Vocalist Group was on the stage. They were good but they were no Limited Warranty.

Finally, it was my time to shine and, although nervous and sober, I walked out onto the stage, wireless microphone in hand, and landed my first joke—to a semitepid response. I had planned a set of my best "single girl in a nightclub" jokes, but as I scanned the crowd and saw mostly families in jean shorts and fanny packs, I got the sinking feeling none of these people had been single or in a bar since VCRs were invented. But I was determined to win them over, so I smiled big and muscled through, managing to elicit a decent laugh on every joke and even a huge applause break on my last bit. The clapping was ear shattering when I said, "Thank you, good night." I hoped Angelina was watching. *See you in the semifinals, bitch!*

Next, it was Keith's turn to take the stage. I waited backstage while people congratulated me. I also gave little Yvette a little pep talk because the poor thing was a bundle of nerves, then I watched the last couple of minutes of Keith's performance on the monitor. I really hoped he'd do well because if you're going to lose, you still want to give a good show. There was a joke about helicopters in there that seemed to go over very well with the crowd and then he called it back at the end, which the audience *loved.*

Keith and I held hands while Ed McMahon asked the judges for my scores. And here's where things took a surreal turn. One by one the four judges turned over their scorecards. My first score was three stars out of four, not too bad, but my second score was two stars—pretty bad—then things went a little fuzzy, but my final score was two-and-a-half stars. Then Keith's scores were read off, and he ended up with something like three-and-a-half stars. Keith was declared the winner, while I stood there paralyzed and humiliated with a frozen smile on my face.

The second we walked through the door of the stage into the backstage area, Keith was immediately surrounded by hoopla and fanfare. If my memory serves me correctly, someone may have baked him a congratulations-on-kicking-Stefanie's-ass during the time between our scores being announced and our arrival backstage. I, on the other hand, was suddenly as popular as a skin rash.

"We're booking your flight home. The next plane leaves at six p.m. There's a bus waiting to take the losing contestants back to the hotel so you can grab your stuff in order to make your plane on time," the travel coordinator said, only glancing up long enough to hand me my "get the hell out of here" printout itinerary.

"I'm kind of hungry. Can I just have a few of those finger sandwiches now?" I asked, seeing as my blood sugar felt at an all-time low. Could I have just caught diabetes from this experience? If so, maybe I could sue.

"We can't let the losing contestants back into the main backstage area, so you'll have to eat something at your hotel or wait for the plane." I didn't get to see little Yvette take the stage, but I gave her a rueful smile before I left. I hoped she would be okay—she was so young and show business was a fickle mistress.

The come-down was difficult, but as I sat on the plane (aisle seat) on the way home, thinking over the events of the past few days, I realized something pretty positive. This business was all about who you know, and I knew Keith—there was a very good chance if he got his own show I could get a job as his driver. I had a perfect driving record.

What Would
Tori Spelling Do?

I have been broken up with a number of times. The first time I ever got my heart truly broken was on an international call to Italy at 3 a.m. My boyfriend, Billy, and I had moved in together in an apartment in Los Angeles, and while I was busy planning our future together, he was busy planning his escape. I probably should've seen it coming, but somehow I wasn't focused on the clues that he was leaving me. Sure, we fought a lot, but didn't lots of couples scream, "Shut the fuck up" at each other? Chet was Billy's best friend, and Billy used him as an alibi on more than one occasion. A couple of times he came home in the middle of the night and when I demanded to know where he'd been, he said, "I was at Denny's counseling Chet on a relationship issue. You know he's having a tough time getting over Heather." Like that was the most normal thing in the world and only a truly insane person would question something so obviously reasonable.

"But why didn't you at least call me?"

"Stefanie," he said in that condescending way people have when they use your name in the conversation. "That would have been rude. Chet was really upset and leaving to make a phone call would have made him feel unimportant." It was as if God lowered a waving red flag from the ceiling telling me Billy was either gay, watching way too much *Oprah,* or most likely screwing someone else. But I let it slide. Sure, he was kind of an asshole, but I was in love and it was easier to believe he loved me, too.

Besides being funny, Billy was the first guy I felt completely comfortable with naked. It's not that I'd never been naked with other men, but I preferred extremely dim lighting where my cellulite would be less likely to be discovered. I'd also perfected a sideways walk that allowed me to get out of bed and sidle out of a room while remaining in silhouette if, God forbid, I had to pee or get dressed to leave. I thought I was pulling off a sort of Mae West move, but apparently it was a bit awkward and it wasn't unusual for the guy to ask, "What's up with the limp?" During extreme body insecurity stretches, I'd been known to hold my pee all night long until I could furtively put my pants back on while still in bed and head to the bathroom—the downside being, after holding it all night, I probably peed louder than a camel. But with Billy, I could lie around buck naked playing chess, drinking beer, and making crank phone calls without feeling self-conscious.

For some people, comfortable may be the kiss of death; for me, it's a drug. Every single morning when we woke up together, even if we'd had a vicious fight the night before, he told me I was beautiful and I chose to go with that. Hey, if a Lean Cuisine tells me it only contains three hundred calories and a third of a gram of fat, who am I to argue, even if it seems way too ridiculously tasty to be true?

One day, a passport arrived for him in the mail. "Why'd you go get a passport?" I asked, truly perplexed. *Doesn't that seem like something you'd mention in casual conversation to the person you live with?*

"Oh, Chet was getting a passport so I decided to go with him for the hell of it and went ahead and got one, too." You didn't need to be Perry Mason to find offering to share an entire afternoon standing in line in a government office suspect. It was like volunteering to work at the DMV.

"Really? 'Cause you never mentioned it," I said, trying to sound casual.

"Jesus, what are you, my parole officer? Do I have to tell you everywhere I go? What's the big deal? It's a passport. I went to keep him company."

"Then why get a passport? That just seems weird."

"You are so needy and paranoid; I can't even deal with you right now." He did have a point there—which just showed how well he knew me, which proved I needed to work harder to keep him around. So I put it out of my mind.

Before I met Billy, I'd been single for a long time. I was incredibly picky, as I called it, or afraid of intimacy, as my therapist called it. I found it tough to find men who didn't annoy me. I'd put the kibosh on a second or third date with men who seemed otherwise nice for reasons that made perfect sense to me, like: Too passionate about bowling, showed up for a date wearing a beret, called me a "special lady," owned every Tom Cruise movie, loved the Starship song, "We Built This City," referred to wine as "vino," counted carbs at every meal, saw no problem with mock turtlenecks, and one who thought that *Three's Company* was breakthrough television.

I felt incredibly lucky to have finally found a guy who was funny, cute, smart, and didn't irritate me by having opinions I didn't share or quirks I didn't find endearing. In my twenties, nonirritating trumped nice. Although, even in my thirties, nice inched up quite a bit but never overtook nonirritating.

A couple of days after the passport incident, the phone rang at 6 a.m. next to my side of the bed. I picked it up, and a woman's voice asked if she could speak with Billy. He took the phone looking sheepish, and said, "Hello? Oh, *hi* . . . uh huh . . . um . . . can I call you when I get into the office in a little bit?" I felt a white heat travel through my entire body. How was he going to talk his way out of this one? Not wanting to support his notion that I was paranoid, I tried to play it cool.

"*Who the fuck was that?!*" I yelled, surprising myself and probably the residents of our entire apartment building.

"It's not what you think," he said, barely reacting to my rage. I hoped not, because what I thought was that the woman on the other line was his secret fiancée and that they were deep in the planning stages of an extravagant wedding to which all of his friends and family were looking forward to, me his live-in girlfriend being the only nagging hangnail holding up the proceedings. The bitch was probably calling because she was freaking out over which calligrapher to go with for the invitations. "I really didn't want to talk to you about this yet because it's very premature, but I guess I have to now." *Premature?* The wedding was probably only a few months away in my estimation.

"That was a woman calling me from Italy about a job I applied for at a television station there."

He was right. It wasn't what I was thinking. It was worse. He was leaving me to move halfway across the world. The asshole wouldn't even be in stalking distance.

"How and when were you planning on telling me this? By calling me from a gelato parlor?" While I was gearing up for a huge fight, Billy had turned over on our futon and was actually thinking he'd go back to sleep. He didn't even seem slightly worried I might stab him.

"I haven't even interviewed yet. It's not something I'm seriously considering. If it was, I would have absolutely told you."

A month later, he was boxing up the rest of his belongings for the shipping company that would be coming to send his things to Rome. Luckily for him, he "happened" to have a passport.

"This doesn't change anything," he said. "We're not breaking up."

"Then why aren't I coming with you?"

"Because," he said, as if explaining to a toddler why she can't have a sixth juice box, "I need to go have an adventure. And you wouldn't have anything to do there." An adventure that would be hampered by a girlfriend tagging along, obviously.

The bastard cried at the airport when I dropped him off. "Take good care of my car for me! Don't forget to start the engine once a week!"

Then I didn't hear from him. This was a pre–cell phone breakup, so it wasn't completely clear to me that we were over until a month later when he finally called from work and said what he'd been saying without saying it from the first three months of our relationship on. "I don't see myself ever marrying you. I've had my doubts for a while." I was devastated. Why I continued starting his car for him once a week is beyond me.

That split left me vulnerable and got the attach/abandon cycle ball rolling. There was the guy who after a couple months of dating—each date initiated by him—left me a five-minute-long message on my voice mail to break things off, which I had the luck of checking while at work.

"Hey, it's Ben. Sorry to leave this on your voice mail, but I just didn't want to see you or I knew I'd just end up changing my mind because you are so damn hot." (Full disclosure: He may not have said the thing about me being hot; I may have added that in my mind in retrospect to take the sting out.) "The thing is, I just don't think I'm up for the type of relationship you seem to want. I have a lot going on in my life, and although I really like you as a person, I simply know I won't be able to meet your needs and will only end up disappointing you. So . . ." It went on and on from there; I wish there'd been an intermission. The funny thing is, I *knew* the relationship was going nowhere. The writing was on the wall, or, actually, on his nightstand in the form of a book called, *Obsessive Love: When It Hurts Too Much to Let Go.* And he wasn't obsessed with *me.*

Then there was Paul, my boyfriend of about four months, whose answering machine did the dirty work of breaking up with me for him. We woke up in his bed one morning to the sound of the phone ringing. He grabbed me, pulling me close for a snuggle, letting the machine get it while he sleepily reached for my breast. Bad move. After his outgoing message played, we both got to hear:

"Hey, babe, just reminding you that we have dinner with my parents tonight. Grab a couple bottles of that Chardonnay they like, will ya? Call me later."

He wasn't the only one who'd be grabbing a couple of bottles of wine for later.

Another guy I'd been dating for the better part of six months showed up on Valentine's Day with a huge bag that did not hide a huge, adorable stuffed panda or a giant chocolate heart but four pounds of laundry he needed me to do because he had to go to Brazil on business for three weeks. I never received one phone call, but I did get a postcard featuring a sunny beach packed with topless girls in bikini bottoms that read, "The weather's beautiful, wish you were here!" It should have read, "The girls are gorgeous, glad you're not here to cock block!" I never heard from him again.

But lest you think I'm a victim, many of these breakups or even failures to score a second date I had coming to me. I can only imagine what their reasons have been, but I'm assuming a few were that I cried on a first date—more than three times; on a double date I once made out with the "other guy"; I've been known to be a bit needy, calling a guy once and then when he didn't call back, calling three more times just to "check in"; and too many talks about "our relationship": "Where is it going?" "Do you see yourself getting married?" "How soon?" Oh, and then there was the time I got drunk and puked on a guy's bath mat. Except he didn't break up with me; he married me.

All this is not to say that I haven't been on the giving end of quite a few "It's over"s myself. My normal passive/aggressive approach to ending a short-term relationship has always been the time-honored practice of just not returning phone calls. I've always felt that it's more humane than saying, "I'm sorry, but due to the fact that on our last date you yelled at the valet, undertipped the waiter, and wore a puka shell necklace, I can no longer imagine you inside me ever again." I've never been great with the face-to-face. I have a friend with a membership to Match.com who goes on first dates like it's her job. Because of this, she's mastered the art of ending a relationship with the precision of a brain surgeon—and the bedside manner. She has no trouble just saying, "Sorry, it's not going to work out.

But I wish you the best. Please don't call me anymore." I once employed her to call a guy I'd been out with on one date and knew I never wanted to see again but who continued to call me over and over. Since I'd only been out with him once, I banked on him not recognizing my voice and had her do it. I hear he took it well.

Another time I actually faked a tonsillectomy that would put me out of commission for weeks in the hopes that the guy I was dating would meet someone new in the meantime. It might have worked if I hadn't run into him a week later at a 7-Eleven buying a six-pack of beer. "It helps with the healing," I said as hoarsely as possible. I suppose I deserved being called a bitch, but really I kind of dodged a bullet. I mean, hey, a guy who can just fly off the handle that easily is someone I'm glad I avoided!

But by far the most dramatic breakup was fortunately the last one before I met my husband.

I'd been trying to end a disastrous nine-month affair for quite a while when it finally culminated with me having to pull a Tori Spelling. This is a maneuver that I learned straight from a Lifetime movie awesomely titled *Mother, May I Sleep with Danger?* starring woman-in-peril Tori Spelling. In the movie, Tori's character falls in love with a guy but then figures out he's totally psycho so she tries to break up with him. Unfortunately, as it often goes with psychos, he doesn't take the news so well and he drugs her, kidnaps her, and hauls her to a cabin in the woods, where, of course, no one can hear her scream. But when Tori comes out of her drug stupor to find psycho berating her for betraying him, she keeps her wits about her and comes up with the perfect ploy: She tells him that she's madly in love with him but that it's her *mother* who's keeping them apart. He and his ever so slightly dysfunctional personality are not the problem at all! This confuses him, like when you hide a tennis ball behind a dog's head and the dog gets disoriented and starts to walk in circles, not knowing what to believe. That's when Tori makes a break for it. Luckily, I had seen the movie fairly recently when I found myself in an emergency situation.

This was one of those relationships that in retrospect makes you question yourself and your judgment. I might as well have been taking a catnap on railroad tracks, thinking, "Surely a train won't be coming by anytime soon." The man in question and I started out as friends but soon found ourselves dating. He called me constantly from the time we started hanging out. My friends found it weird, but I found having a guy I was really into calling me ten times a day to be sort of cool and intense. He wasn't codependent; he just needed to know my schedule! He was just thinking about me! He had a funny thing to tell me! Of course, there's a fine line between "a little too into me" and "a fucking lunatic." He was always a moody guy, either brooding for days and drinking way too much, or full of manic energy, planning Vegas getaways at the spur of the moment and drinking way too much. At first I found his moods sexy and interesting, mistaking his brooding as existential angst—when in actuality he was just out of Vicodin. I also sometimes mistook his giddy moods as being extra in love with me when really he was just excited that he'd gotten away with shoplifting.

It took way too long to realize we were on a downward spiral, but as he became less and less stable, I found the only mood of his I could tolerate was sleeping. One morning, as he lay in bed snoring louder than a rusty leaf blower, I tiptoed around, collecting my things, hoping to make a clean getaway. Unfortunately, he woke up hungover and suspicious. I told him as nicely as I could that he was completely out of his mind and that I was done with him for good, and continued heading for the exit. Suddenly he flipped out and tried to stop me from leaving him by physically blocking his front door while ranting and raving; I guess he was thinking that if I spent some time as a hostage, I might choose to use my time in captivity recognizing all his wonderful qualities. It was about that moment I realized I was not just in a dead-end relationship but I might actually be in danger.

That's when I had the brilliant idea to pull the Tori Spelling.

I spoke gently as you might to a gorilla if you accidentally fell into its cage. "You know what? You're right. I am crazy to let someone as amazing as you go. I'm just really stressed lately and obviously taking it out on you. You don't deserve that." It was working. He started pacing back and forth, telling me he was relieved to hear that I realized this was my problem and not his.

"You're just mixed up, confused."

"Right," I said. "Why don't I go home and give some

thought to why I have been acting like such an unreasonable and selfish bitch." He noticeably perked up.

"Yeah, yeah, you should do that. And then we can get together later tonight."

"Absolutely." And I got the hell out. Sure enough, Tori came through. I guess for him I was literally the one that got away.

Live Nude Girls

Anytime I hear an Ani DiFranco song, I can't help but think about vaginas. It's midnight. Somehow I've ended up at a lesbian bar in West Hollywood surrounded by women. Suddenly, out of nowhere, my idol, Ani DiFranco, saunters in, jumps on stage, and starts giving an impromptu acoustic performance. I manage to fight my way through a smoky haze of flannel shirts and wallet chains, getting closer and closer to Ani, and finally scoring the one empty seat directly in front of the stage. As I'm letting myself get wrapped up in her passion, I get the strong sense that she's singing directly to me—every steel string guitar chord change, every erotic lyric—and as I look around I realize the stone-washed-jeans crowd is looking at me with jealousy because she *is* singing directly to me. My face gets hot, I try to play it cool, but Ani unquestionably sings at me hungrily.

The minute her set is over, she makes a beeline to my chair. "I'm Ani," she says. "Who are *you?*"

We sit at the bar, drinking about thirty Kahlúa and Creams, talking about everything and nothing. Before I know it, we're making out heavily, so heavily the bartender in her Violent Femmes T-shirt and six nose rings tells us to wrap it up. But Ani is nowhere near ready for the night to end, and she demands that I come back to her place for a nightcap. I'm terrified but enormously curious and titillated, so I agree—and before I can change my mind, we're whisked up to Ani's Hollywood Hills pad in the back of a random fan's Jeep Wrangler.

Once out of the car, Ani grabs my hand and guides me up the steep incline of steps to her funky Spanish-style house. Holding hands and giggling like naughty schoolgirls, we fall lustfully into a hammock swing on her porch and continue our make-out session surrounded by dozens of colorful hand-painted statues and intricately woven hanging baskets. Ani slowly caresses me as we lie in moonlight. Every now and again she pours me wine from a nearby bottle of Italian Chianti and we feed each other succulent summer fruits from one of the baskets: cherries, kiwis, red grapes, and papaya. After a while, Ani breaks our lip-lock and gets up to grab one of her many guitars lined up just inside her French doors, giving me a chance to gaze at her marvelous womanly curves. She turns, catching me staring, smiles, and comes back to the swing.

"You're shivering," she says in a raspy whisper.

"I'm not cold," I say back, voice quivering. Gently she

covers me with an ancient crocheted afghan and strums me an ode to my reproductive rights that is so exquisite I make her swear she'll put it on her next CD.

"Of course. And I'll dedicate it to you. To this night."

Suddenly, Ani puts down her guitar, rips off the afghan, and kisses me more and more ardently, moving deliberately southward . . . unbuttoning my pants . . . and *that's as far as that fantasy goes.*

Like most women, I have fantasized about a little girl-on-girl action, but even my wildest imagination stays G-rated, only culminating at second base—under the shirt, over the bra. In fantasy and reality, my mouth has never been anywhere close to another woman's nether regions. But I *have* looked.

Years ago, my friend Nina lived a mere two blocks from Crazy Girls, one of the more notorious topless joints in Hollywood. Despite the proliferation of titty bars in cities across the USA (in Texas, I believe there are more strip clubs than strip malls) and despite the glittering lights and flashing signs practically yelling NUDE, NUDE, NUDE three times so that you can't possibly miss the fact that there are indeed naked ladies in there, neither one of us had ever gone to one.

But all that changed the night of Nina's thirtieth birthday.

A group of us, including her boyfriend at the time, were hanging out in her one-bedroom apartment, sloppy drunk on Veuve Clicquot, dancing around the living room and trying to remember the last verse to *The Golden Girls'* theme song.

"Thank you for bein' a friennnd, traveled down the road and back again, your heart is true, you're a pal and a confidant. And if you . . . ," our friend Mel warbled.

"Yeah, we know that part, but what's the next verse? Something about 'I hope it will always be this way' shit!" The guy who came up with Google had the audacity not to have invented it yet, so we were reduced just to singing the part we knew over and over, when someone interrupted our repeat performance by suggesting we hit Crazy Girls. Okay, I think that someone was me. But the idea caught fire like a Pinto backed into a wall, and just like that we went from Golden Girls to Crazy Girls in the space of five minutes.

By the time we'd walked over and were paying our admission—well, truth be told, only the men ended up having to pay (somehow, if you're a woman accompanied by men it's easy to haggle, and by haggle I mean show a glimpse of cleavage)—I was giddy with excitement. We were about to finally venture past the bacteria-laden black curtain dividing nakedness from the rest of the civilized world.

A huge bouncer with his head shaved to a shine opened the drapes and beckoned us through and Nina and I headed straight to the bar so that we could check things out from the safety of a close proximity to alcoholic beverages. Once I had a seven-dollar Captain Morgan's and Diet Coke in my hand, I took it all in. On the main stage was a gorgeous brunette in a tiny, sparkly G-string named "Stormy" with the exact body type I've always wanted but could never achieve unless I had a full body transplant, which I'm pretty sure has only been attempted once in India on a sheep. She had long legs like a pony, and slim, boyish hips with the slight curve of the lower back that made her butt stick out like a pout—a butt without a trace of cellulite—bitch! Sure, she was sexy as hell, but I found myself fixating on how hard she must have to work out to have a body like that.

"What's up with that dancer's amazing ass?" I asked Nina, who was ogling Destiny, a blonde on the second stage. I hadn't even known Nina was into blondes!

"Yeah, she does look great. She's clearly trained as a dancer her whole life. But what about Destiny? Do you think her boobs are real?" Looking at Destiny's two overfilled water balloons trying to burst free of her chest cavity, I didn't even dignify Nina's question with a response. I turned my attention back to Stormy. *Had she spent her childhood dedicating herself to hours of ballet, determined to become a prima ballerina, but due to an ugly ankle injury ended up on the pole? Also, how much did she have to work out?* I figured since she had her days free she could pretty much live at the gym. The glare of the lights was making it difficult to gauge her actual physical perfection, so needing to get a closer look, I left my bar stool and sat down at the foot of the stage—and remained there until I'd exhausted my entire paycheck. Luckily, there was an ATM on the premises that dispensed one-dollar bills. These strip clubs, they're always thinking!

The whole vibe was completely different than I'd anticipated. I half-expected to see women sobbing while forcing themselves to strip off their tops in a last-ditch attempt not to get evicted from their housing projects or pay the government twenty thousand dollars in back taxes. But these women did not look unhappy in the least. The sex in the air was palpable. The driving beat of rap music combined with topless, gyrating, beautiful women, and adding quite a nice alcohol buzz to the mix, in short, made me incredibly horny. Clearly, most men felt the same way, except a few, I'm assuming regulars, who were clustered around small circular tables, sipping Jack Daniel's while getting a lap dance, acting like they were just conducting a business meeting, and not like they had a big old set of knockers in their face.

At first I found it a turn-on to be around so many aroused men. But before long, I was getting suckered into the appeal of each girl who took the stage, choosing favorites and cheering them on. Needing, wanting them to notice me and pay me special attention—which they did. And I'm positive it was because they really liked me. I know in my heart it had nothing to do with their car payments.

Nina and I went back again and again. We became like addicts in need of a nudie fix. Oh, sure, we'd *try* to go out to other places, parties, and bars, but it seemed like we always ended up at Crazy Girls before the night was over. And so we became regulars. Crazy Girls was kind of like our Cheers but with hotter waitresses. We even got sucked into some of the club drama, tearing up when we heard that Venus's girlfriend broke up with her because she couldn't accept her job and recommending a lawyer friend when Trinity got pinched for shoplifting. We knew that our favorite stripper, Crystal, a skinny, honey blonde with a major heroin problem, was in danger of getting fired. Some nights she would look stunning and sit with us for a while to talk, while other nights she would be nodding out in a corner with a couple of guys who looked like they had priors. I would've tried to help, but short of paying her for a few lap dances, what could I do? I'm not Mother Teresa.

One night Crystal floated the idea of either Nina or me cosigning a credit card for her to help her get out of the business. Cosign a credit card? Was she insane? I was, of course, appalled. Why would she want to *stop stripping?* With a body like that—she was the hottest girl there. I couldn't be a party to Crazy Girls losing its best girl. It just felt wrong.

Around this time, Nina and I agreed that it was probably time to kick it up a notch and experience the Totally Nude strip bar. After all, I was starting to get desensitized to the whole topless experience. So one night while at a party, willing ourselves to be out among people without the social lubricant of naked breasts, we casually mentioned to a couple of guys that we'd never been to an all-nude strip club.

Ten minutes later, we arrived at the Star Strip on La Cienega Boulevard—XXX-All-Nude Girls, Girls, Girls again, in case we weren't sure what type of nudity we'd be in for. Right away, it was clear we were in trouble. It was like we'd tripped into another universe, and I'd seen enough *Twilight Zone*s to know that this probably wouldn't end well. After paying a twenty-dollar admission, we were led over to seats— which, for some reason, the personnel had neglected to cover in plastic—in front of the stage for what was basically vaginas on parade. The men panting over the girls on stage were not here to discuss any sort of business. The only business that was being conducted here was the business of vagina. These girls didn't even bother dancing. They barely sauntered across the stage only to lie down on their back two seconds later, rip off their G-string, and splay their legs apart, like a puppy looking for a belly rub.

I couldn't understand the appeal whatsoever. I mean, I already owned one of those bad boys. With a mirror and a slightly uncomfortable squatting position, I could see it anytime I wanted to and be twenty dollars richer for it (although I did enforce a two-drink minimum on myself), but unless I'm shaving, I try to avoid viewing that area as much as possible.

These women were proudly putting their goods in our faces, I think hoping our dates would give them more money. Nina and I, out of pure guilt that they were degrading themselves, kept the dollars coming. But it was a catch-22; the more money we gave them, the more into it they thought we were and the more unwanted attention we got. When the hoo-hoos got too close for comfort, we tried to make awkward conversation.

"Hey, Mercedes, where'd you get those Lucite heels?" Nina asked. "They're really nice!" Mercedes didn't miss a beat.

"Oh, Frederick's of Hollywood. It's literally across the street. You wouldn't believe it, but they're not even that uncomfortable," she said as if we were just chatting over a bathroom stall and not staring straight at her clit piercing.

We might've had an easier time getting through it, but Nina and I were way too sober, seeing as how it was illegal to serve alcohol when the girls were completely naked. I thought it should be illegal *not* to serve alcohol. Right then and there, I vowed to be completely liquored up the next time I was subjected to viewing women's private parts. This might be tough to do in the gym locker room, but somehow I'd make it work.

Although we were desperate to leave, we knew the guys had dropped eighty dollars to get us all in, so we figured we should be polite and give it a few more minutes. I tried to think about other things, like the science of stripper names. *Why is Mercedes a good stripper name but Hummer not so much? You could name yourself after a whisky, like Black Velvet, but I don't think Old Crow would go over nearly as well. Jasmine, sure, Flytrap, doubtful.* That burned off about five minutes. Then I spent another five minutes just trying to avoid eye contact with the other clientele. I needn't have worried too much because all eyes were glued to the spread out on stage. Men with their eyes glazed over, practically hypnotized by the pussy.

I was done—I needed to get out of there immediately. But as I was grabbing my purse and throwing down a good-bye buck, Asia came out to perform, strutting her way down the narrow strip of stage to an *amazing* song. I desperately wanted to leave without seeing one more vagina, but I had to know who was singing, so I waited for Asia to get close enough to ask.

The next day I went straight out and bought my first Ani DiFranco CD for the song "32 Flavors."

It's been years since I've been inside a strip club, but to this day all I need is to hear Ani's voice and I'm right back there like it was yesterday.

How I Met
Your Father

I was walking down Franklin Avenue in Los Angeles with my two funny, pretty friends, Suzy and Bonnie, lamenting our single status, wondering why it was so hard to meet a decent guy, when we spotted a girl we all knew in passing. This girl was a "little person" who stood no more than three feet tall in heels. She was also about twenty pounds overweight, which on a little person is not something a few minutes on the Stairmaster can take care of, and her eyebrows were a mess. But, there she was with her husband. We all watched with fascination while her good-looking, normal-size spouse patiently helped her out of their van customized for her height-challenged stature and occasional wheelchair use. It was clear to us that he was enamored with her—Suzy, Bonnie, and I didn't even have casual sex possibilities.

"God!" Suzy said. "We must be such cunts."

I had been single for the better part of my twenties and early thirties. When I was alone and complaining, I got a lot of shitty advice—especially from friends of mine who were already coupled up. "You'll meet the right person when you're ready." What does that even mean? How does one get ready to meet someone? Are there exercises? Quizzes? Can I hire a tutor?

"You always find someone when you're not looking." Really? 'Cause I'd bet that billionaire who invented Match.com would let out a huge laugh right now. Am I just supposed to wait for the boyfriend fairy to drop a cute, smart, nerdy Jewish guy on my doorstep while I'm in my sweats lying on the couch crying over an episode of Discovery's *Health Miracles*? And then there's my personal favorite, "You have to love yourself before anyone can love you." Well, I happen to know many people who can't stand themselves and have still managed to find someone who begs to differ with them.

I cried at quite a few weddings in my life, not out of happiness for the couple but sadness for myself. Let's not get into specifics; crying is crying, so I'm sure the brides were unaware and probably didn't miss me when I spent half the reception alone in the bathroom sulking, so I seriously doubt it took anything out of their special day. And if it did bother any of you that I was sobbing louder than your mother while you said your vows, maybe you shouldn't have been such a stickler about me bringing a "plus one."

So, I'd heard all the bad advice and more while spending

the better part of my prime hoping the right guy was going to happen along while I was too busy loving myself to notice. When I did finally meet the man I eventually married, one of my friends said, "Good for you. You did the work on yourself and the right guy came into your life." Wrong. I did eventually find "the one" but I credit luck, AOL, and some particularly bad dates with other people for my husband, Jon. I didn't suddenly develop a better, more evolved personality.

In the old days of the Internet, everyone had AOL—sadly, I still do, mostly because I'm deathly afraid of change, not because I like AOL. But back then we were a proud community; we felt we belonged to one of the first networking sites and we filled out our member profiles, listing our hobbies, jobs, marital status, and age, with great gusto.

It just so happened that I enjoyed looking up these member profiles, finding people who were online at the time and then sending them a random instant message along the lines of "Hi, I'm seventy-five years young and looking for a good time. You game?" Usually the recipient of my communication either completely ignored me or immediately asked for my height/weight/pic, which is gross. Come on, I'm seventy-five!

One night I found the profile of a guy who said he was in television and he listed his hobbies as "sleep." If there's one thing I like, it's a person with few to no hobbies, so I decided to mess with him. I instant-messaged him: "Hey, I see on your profile that you're in television and I'm thinking of buying a new one. Do you have any tips?" He responded: "I've always been partial to Toshiba." *Yes, a sense of humor!*

And with that we started a daily banter that went on for four months, building into a full-fledged relationship in my mind. It was the classic story of girl meets boy online, girl flirts with boy, boy doesn't want to meet girl because he believes she may resemble a short, chain-smoking Fran Lebowitz. But every night we'd instant-message while finishing work from our day, sorting laundry, watching television—like a couple, who had never met.

> STEF: I have big news.
>
> JON: Spill it, dammit.
>
> STEF: I bought new sheets with really high thread count. They are unbelievable. I feel so adult, though. I never saw myself as the type of person who would put a lot of thought into buying sheets.
>
> JON: I nearly fell on my ass for that? But, hey, sheets are important.
>
> STEF: Wha'd you expect?
>
> JON: Pre-op transsexual would have amortized the fall.
>
> STEF: Tell me something revealing about yourself.
>
> JON: I just have that tour with Up with People and a lost weekend with Frank Gifford. But the sheets thing is pretty big. Hey, at seventy-five years old, you need all the creature comforts you can get.

Although we had this great rapport online, he never asked to see a picture, let alone meet me, which, at first, I loved but after a while I found it a little annoying. So, in the meantime,

I continued to date people who had an interest in seeing me in the flesh.

I met Fredrik, a German architecture student in a local pub. We talked for a while and in spite of the fact that he drove a 1970s-style, fully carpeted VW Bus that smelled like it may have transported a dead body at some point in time, he seemed mildly interesting and didn't mind that I asked him straight-out if as a German he still felt bad about the Jews. He was intelligent and, for me, intelligence overrode the bad car. But on our first date, I discovered he resided in a youth hostel, where he rented one small room and shared a bathroom with the other seventeen residents, and drank wine out of a coffee mug despite the fact that he was in his thirties. The lack of any sort of stemware I could live with, but, having a bashful bladder as it was, there was no way I'd be peeing at his place *ever*, which is sort of a deal breaker.

I agreed to a second date strictly to prove to myself that I'm not a snob. But I did insist that he come to my place because I didn't want to smell like his VW until my next shower. At the end of what was an awkward evening, where I discovered that his sense of humor was best suited to write funny coffee mug slogans, he told me he couldn't see me again because "your apartment has very bad lines, architecturally speaking" and "I don't see myself with someone long-term who doesn't have an eye for aesthetics." Even though I was relieved, I did fight the urge to yell, "You live in a fucking youth hostel. You are forced to pee with people who are not your friends!" Jesus, my two-bedroom, two-bath apartment (thank you, rent control) a block from the beach *had* to be a slight step up.

That night I instant-messaged with Jon for hours and we made fun of Fredrik for most of it. I knew I was falling for him. There was just the slight problem that he had yet to express a desire to meet. But, if I went out with someone else, I'd feel like I was cheating on him a little bit, which was crazy!

> JON: Where have you been?
> STEF: Knocking on doors, trying to give folks some pamphlets on the Lord Jehovah.
> JON: I just sent you an email.
> STEF: I just opened it. Should I read it now?
> JON: No—hang on till Passover.
> STEF: Please, I'm gonna wait till Purim. You must be missing me like crazy.
> JON: Liquor can't kill the pain. What are you doing tomorrow?
> STEF: Are you asking me out?
> JON: Ha ha. I'm going to spend my weekend sleeping.
> STEF: You are a pain in the ass.

So while the man of my dreams slept, I moved on to the next guy who had a few things working against him from the get-go, starting with the spelling of his name, which was Geoffrey. Geoffrey was a member of a Smoked Fish of the Month club. The night he pulled some dehydrated carp out of his closet, I pretty much knew I never wanted to see his penis. I went out with Geoffrey very casually a couple more times strictly out of boredom, but his annoying qualities were adding up faster than a guest list for a Greek wedding. So, even though I knew I was completely done and would have much rather stayed home on my computer with my real boyfriend, I had to go out with Geoffrey one more time because I'd agreed much earlier to go to a big party with him and I felt bad canceling right before.

Our last date was an unmitigated disaster. He picked me up for the party and immediately tried to dress me up a little more. "Aren't you a little casual?" Jesus. Jon would have never made a comment about my outfit. Jon liked me exactly how I was. "Maybe you could put on a skirt?" With a name like Geoffrey, I should've known he'd have a little fashion advice up his sleeve.

I wasn't a stranger to industry parties and I was pretty sure I knew how to dress, but at this point, I just wanted to get through it even if it meant putting on my high school prom dress to make this douche happy.

Naturally, every woman at the party was in jeans. Geoffrey continued to annoy me by making pompous comments and eating the last of the brownies. I was embarrassed, pissed, and just wanted to go home and be with Jon.

Luckily, the house was only a five-minute drive from my apartment. But when we got to my place, even though I was ready to drop and roll out of the car while it was still moving, Geoffrey told me he was too drunk to drive and could he please just come up and have a cup of coffee. So I let him up.

Cue sinister music. "Could I just lie in your bed for a few minutes? I just need to sober up before I drive home."

"Fine." I didn't want to be responsible for him on the road, but it didn't mean I had to talk to him.

I lay in my bed with Geoffrey fully dressed, wishing he would go home so I could check my email. I almost started drifting off, but I was distracted by a distinct and repetitive thumping noise. It was steady at first but then picked up a little bit. Did I dare glance over? Big mistake. Geoffrey had furtively removed most of his clothes and was lying in his boxer shorts abusing himself. *This can't be. There is no way this guy is masturbating in my bed! How could he be doing that when he knows I hate him?* I turned away and suddenly, without warning, I felt a warm splat on my hip.

"What the fuck? Are you out of your mind? You just came on my hip! Get out!"

"Sorry," he said, sheepishly. Like a three-year-old who got caught putting glitter glue on the leather chair.

"Get. Out. Now." He dutifully put on his pants and left my apartment. And that's when I went online, saw my guy waiting up for me, and promptly asked his ass out.

STEF: You are meeting me for coffee. This is ridiculous.

JON: Um, well, this week is pretty bad. How about next week?

STEF: Fine. Coffee Bean and Tea Leaf on Montana. Next Tuesday, 9 a.m.

JON: Okay, I'll have a red backpack with me.

I knew I was in love with this guy and I refused to endure one more date with any other men, men who could spurt on my hip with no warning.

The day before our coffee date, I started getting excited. This was going to be a pivotal moment of my life! Just think of the possibilities. AOL would probably want to sponsor our wedding, seeing as how it was highly likely we were their very first success story. Members meeting and marrying based on a silly profile. I wondered if he'd end up proposing to me online—maybe in an email or instant message? I went online and checked out wedding invitations that had a "computer theme."

The night before the meeting, I started getting monu-mentally nervous. I changed clothes until there was a huge cliché pile on my bed, 'cause how does a person dress to meet the love of her life at *9 a.m.*? You can't really show off body parts or wear a ton of makeup; you have to feign a "this is how I look every day at work kind of vibe," which is tough unless you're a Vegas casino cocktail waitress or perhaps a swimwear model. Also, I wondered if there were any diets that would allow me to lose ten pounds overnight. I'd already eaten din-ner but I figured I'd at least try to fast for the next eight hours while I was sleeping.

The next morning, I'd finally settled on black pants and a red shirt (red is a confidence color) and decided to get there twenty minutes early so I could stake out a good seat to see him come in. *Would we start making out immediately? Would we play it cool? Would we at least hold hands?*

When I arrived, there was a young guy sitting outside with a maroon, definitely not red, backpack on the chair next to him. He was cute in a Jonathan Taylor Thomas way, definitely not the nerdy Jew with whom I imagined a life together. So, I bypassed maroon backpack guy and went in to grab a coffee before securing a seat to look for my new boyfriend. After a few minutes of not seeing any red backpacks coming in, I had an unnerving thought: What if the baby-faced guy is him?

"Excuse me, are you Jon?" I sort of half whispered, since the thought of anyone thinking this was a blind date was less than appealing.

"Stefanie?" he said. He had a sexy voice—in spite of not being my type. But it was awkward. He was a real person. And having never seen a picture of him, I was completely unnerved.

We made small talk for an hour while I nervously obsessed on how strange it was to be sitting face-to face with the man I'd spoken to like a lover for four months. He didn't seem as disconcerted by the situation as I was, but considering his expectations had been almost nonexistent, he had nowhere to go but up. So, when he walked me to my car and said, "I'm better over drinks and during the later hours of the day. Can I call you?" I wasn't sure what to do. Damn, I'd been talking to the guy online for months, so how could I just say "no, thanks" without him thinking I was making that decision based on his looks, which weren't bad at all. He was actually sort of hot, just not what I expected. Plus, I figured it would be best to break our engagement face-to-face—luckily, I'd had enough sense not to actually put the order through on the invites, since the printing charge was nonrefundable.

"Sure. That would be great."

That Friday night, I found myself having a few beers with Jon at a dive bar in Hollywood. We sat across from each other and talked about jobs, music, politics—all the first-date classics. It was nice. He was polite, funny, sweet. The time sort of flew by, and suddenly it was 1 a.m. and time to go. I saw no reason to point out that now that we were face-to-face I didn't think we could get married. *This is just two people grabbing a few beers together. It's not even a date, officially.* An official date involved food was how I rationalized my plans to avoid telling him the wedding was off.

When Jon dropped me off at the end of the night, I said a quick, "Thanks for the beers" and hopped out of the car before he could even respond.

That night there was an email from Jon asking me out for sushi. *Shit, food.* But when I came online, we instant-messaged and he was just as hilarious and comfortable as always—which made what I had to do even more devastating.

I figured it wouldn't kill me to go out with him once more. It wasn't like I wasn't having a good time with him—it just wasn't an *online* good time.

I had trouble relaxing during our second date. Although there was a copious amount of sake consumed, I couldn't shake the weirdness that was being with Jon in person. He was too real, too present, too interested in what I had to say.

I felt standoffish and generally not myself. After dinner, we went for a drink, after which Jon pointed out that I flirted with a guy at the bar. I maintained that I wasn't *flirting*, I was just interested in hearing more about his "sculpting studio." After all, the movie *Ghost* had only been out for nine years, so pottery wheels were still a titillating topic. Plus, Jon wasn't my boyfriend! We were ex-fiancées—although I hadn't alerted him *just yet.*

When Jon took me home at the end of the night, I amateurishly hadn't thought to take my seat belt off before pulling up to the front of my building, so when he went in for a good night kiss, I was stuck. I kissed him back for a minute or two, surprising the hell out of myself. Then without warning, I started channeling Blanche from *The Golden Girls*, a southern belle who although caught up in the passion was trying her best to remain a respectable lady. "Oh, my, my, *my*!" I said, just barely avoiding a stagey accent. "I really must go. It's so late and if I stay any longer who knows *what* kind of trouble I might get myself into! Good night!" And I again hopped out of the car and into the safety of my apartment. Alone. Totally good. Relieved. Scared shitless.

I don't know for sure why I went through with the third date. I could've cancelled. I've certainly done it countless times before. Almost every time I've felt genuine fear of letting someone get too close to me, I've bailed—giving myself almost any rationalization. But, somehow with Jon, I just couldn't find one.

We were walking silently down the Santa Monica Promenade when Jon stopped and looked at me. "Look, maybe this is weird for you. It's weird for me, too. Maybe I'm an idiot to keep asking you out. But I'm still the same guy you talked to on the computer for months. I'm still him." Whoa, he called my shit out. "I don't know. Maybe you could pretend there's a keyboard between us."

Sitting at dinner over a glass of wine, something shifted ever so slightly. Maybe it was the booze or maybe it was the candlelight, but he was pretty damn cute. Which was not my imagination, since the waiter was clearly flirting with him. He must've offered Jon more pepper on his salad than any waiter in the history of Caesar salad service.

"Um, the waiter's flirting with you," I pointed out.

"No, he's not. The man just really knows his way around a peppermill."

He was funny, he was smart, he was nice, and I was suddenly feeling lucky to be with him.

Sitting in the dark theater watching *The Muse,* because I love Albert Brooks and anyone I date better love him, too, I started itching for him to hold my hand. I looked over at his hand sitting placidly in his lap. He had great hands. *God, why doesn't he touch me already? What's the holdup? Doesn't he like me? Did I screw it up? I thought he liked me. Maybe I read the signals wrong. Hold my hand, asshole.* Ever so slowly, as if he was reading my mind, his hand reached over and took mine. And then he leaned over and whispered in my ear, "This movie sucks." There was no denying it. The movie absolutely sucked, and I was absolutely falling in love.

Bigs and Littles

When I was almost thirty years old, my friend Samantha talked me into being a camp counselor with her to a group of thirteen-year-old girls at a YMCA camp. Samantha was a major do-gooder, always up for getting out and volunteering for causes usually involving animals or kids or the elderly. I considered myself more of a mental do-gooder. I had good intentions but preferred community service I could do from my couch while reading magazines and eating takeout—kind of like *The Secret* but with trans fats.

But this actually sounded sort of fun to me—specifically because I had great memories of summer camp and because I'd be with the thirteen-year-old group, which I felt was my target demo. Hell, I was practically like a thirteen-year-old girl myself with my love of Gummi bears, shopping at Forever 21, and illegally downloading Britney Spears songs—except that I lived in my own apartment, had a job, and had slightly easier access to alcohol. So I quickly agreed to do it, and before I knew what happened, I was a few hundred miles from home at a camp by Big Bear Lake getting to know my young charges. As I quickly found out, a lot had changed since I was thirteen. Today's thirteen-year-olds were smoking pot and, as it turns out, very, very over Britney Spears. They preferred hard-core rap. And out of twelve girls, at least ten of them had names that were some version of Kristine.

As soon as I'd hit cabin nine and laid my knapsack and boom box down on my steel bunk, the girls started sussing me out.

"Do you like rap?" an impossibly tall African-American girl named Cristal wanted to know. *Are thirteen-year-olds supposed to be seven feet tall?* I wondered. *Would it be rude to ask her if she played basketball?* I thought it might be. I mean, it should be obvious she did, right? Or, at the very least, volleyball.

"Sure. I love rap."

"Are you down with Mobb Deep?" asked Krissy, an overly smiley girl with strawberry blonde pigtails and braces. I had a bad feeling her mother sent her out on commercial auditions.

"Mobb Deep? I'm not familiar with her work but I love Tupac."

"Mobb Deep isn't a her. And Tupac? He's dead."

"That may be true but it hasn't stopped him from putting out album after album." The guy was more prolific from up in heaven than I'd been my entire life on earth.

"Album? What's an album?"

"It's like a CD only . . . hey, we're due in the mess hall for breakfast and I hear they're serving banana waffles," I said in a voice that reminded me of a preschool teacher.

"I don't eat waffles," yelled a different Crissy from across the room. "I only like plain toast with I Can't Believe It's Not Butter zero calorie spray. I brought my own." If her goal weight was that of an anorexic flamingo, she'd already attained it. But I didn't think this was the right time for a lecture on eating disorders, especially since I could've stood to lose a few pounds. Maybe she'd lend me some of her spray.

Despite the fact that these girls were clearly more mature than I was, I tried to make the most of my two-week session: I attempted to rock climb (getting an avulsion fracture on my ankle in the process), watched them water-ski from my perch on the dock where I iced and elevated my ankle, and made an only semimangled lanyard keychain in arts and crafts. To get on my campers' good side, I purposely "forgot" when it was our night for cleanup duty after dinner, and pretended not to notice when they dressed in clothes that even the Bratz dolls would have deemed "too slutty." Didn't their parents supervise their packing? Did they *have* parents?

When the girls decided to run a massage booth at the camp carnival, I realized I would have to stop trying to be their best friend and become more of a role model/parental figure. While the younger kids did water-balloon throwing and face painting, my girls wanted to put out mattresses to give out back rubs. The male counselors and campers lined up in droves before I put a quick stop to it. To my amazement, the camp administration saw nothing weird about our booth. My girls may have thought I was a buzz kill, but I felt proud that already in my new leadership role I'd saved them from a life of prostitution. Clearly, handing out back rubs at thirteen is a gateway to giving full body massages, which is inches away from working in a downtown massage parlor offering full release. They'd thank me later.

I decided it was time to turn their attention to the end-of-session talent competition. I busted my ass choreographing a dance number to Anita Ward's "You Can Ring My Bell," which they'd never heard of but thankfully liked. "It's cool 'cause it's so old!" said one of the girls whose name started with a K.

"Thanks, Kristen. It's called disco."

"It's *Kir*sten, not Kristen."

I forced them to practice over and over. I was like the Paula Abdul to their Laker Girls. And when they took their victory lap after taking first place in the talent show, I wept like a premenstrual chick watching *Titanic* and they completely ignored me like the thirteen-going-on-thirty teenagers they were. Then they snuck out and smoked a joint behind their cabin, which I pretended not to smell. But when the bus took us all back to the YMCA building where their parents were waiting to pick them up, a few of them gave me a hug and told me I was their favorite counselor. And only one of them furtively gave me the finger. I may have been in a bit over my head, but deep down, I knew I was onto something.

So the following year when Do-gooder told me she was going to apply to be part of the Big Sister program, I was all over it. But I figured as a Big Sister I should set my sights a little younger. Maybe a newborn.

At the orientation, I sat smugly on my school chair with the little desk. I'd always suspected I was a good person, but my decision to become a Big Sister confirmed it for me. Here I was taking the time out of my busy schedule to fill out a mountain of paperwork, get interviewed, and pay fifty bucks for the organization to run a criminal background check on me and even submit my boyfriend to a background check (which I would've paid a hundred for). But I knew this was nothing compared to the personal rewards I would be getting back in spades. I couldn't wait to start enriching a disadvantaged youth's life! I wanted the personal satisfaction I was sure to get from "*expanding horizons through one-on-one friendships*" as the official website advertised.

Once I was cleared to be what they refer to as a "Big" in the program, I'd be matched to a "Little" based on location and compatibility. Sort of like Match.com for nonblood-related siblings who don't plan on screwing. The volunteer went on to give us some tips for success on forming a relationship with your new "Little." According to the program, Littles are pleased as punch just to have a new friend, so there is no need to do things that cost a lot of money. In fact, playing a board game, sharing a pizza with only one topping, taking a walk in the park, or just hanging out and talking were perfect activities. I didn't quite see how if I was a Little I'd be impressed with my Big taking me for a walk in the park to chitchat for an hour. They were clearly underestimating my creativity, possibly used to dealing with amateurs, not seasoned camp counselors like myself, so I cut them some slack.

Next, we went over the ground rules; a commitment of seeing your Little at least once a week—if possible, communication with your Little's parents and checking in with your caseworker every so often for a progress report—sounded easy enough to me. All this "business" was making me fidgety, though. I couldn't wait to get this show on the road. I imagined getting cards and letters from my Little years after our experience, telling me what a huge positive influence I'd been on her. Maybe she'd follow in my footsteps and become a writer and dedicate her first novel to me: "To Stefanie, My Big, the person responsible for opening my eyes to all I could become in life. I couldn't have done this without you." Or, maybe we'd accidentally lose touch and years later I'd be contacted by a producer from *The Montel Williams Show* and told that a certain Little had been thinking about me for years and called the show to help reunite with me, her long-lost Big. I wiped away an anticipatory tear.

A few weeks later, to my great excitement, I was assigned a Little. It was on! Her name was Ashley, she was nine, and the first time I called I got her mother, Patrice, on the phone. "Hi. Is this Patrice?"

"Yes."

"This is Stefanie. I've been assigned to be your daughter's Big Sister. I'm really excited to—"

"*Ashley Lynn!* Pick up the phone!" her mom yelled half into my ear, leaving a slight ringing sensation.

"Who is it?" I heard a voice from far away.

"It's your Big Sister. Just pick up the damn phone." A minute or two went by while I absently flipped through my mail.

"Hello?" said a slightly dour voice.

"Hi, Ashley. This is Stefanie, your new Big. How are you doing?"

"Fine, I guess." I tried to engage her in a little small talk and found that she was not exactly forthcoming over the phone. But, hey, she was probably just shy, not used to people taking such a keen interest in her—or maybe just not really a phone person. I refused to let that dampen my enthusiasm. I'd loosen her up. I'm great at bringing people out of their shells. Especially after a couple of cocktails. I made plans to see her that coming weekend.

Ashley was cute, and with her brown hair, brown eyes, and baseball cap she sort of looked like me. "Hey, it looks like I really could be your big sister," I said.

"Well, maybe my mother." I chose to let that one go. She probably didn't know what I meant. Instead, I focused on how cool she was dressed. She was decked out in a red Adidas sweatsuit and was sporting a fairly new pair of Air Jordans. I immediately complimented her on her outfit.

"My last Big Sister got it for me. The shoes, too."

"Oh, really?" I tried to keep the edge out of my voice. "You had a Big Sister before me?"

"Terry. She's *real* cool. She took me to Magic Mountain." *Great.* There was already an ex in the picture I had to compete with. I really wasn't in the market to become a nine-year-old's sugar daddy.

"What happened to Terry?"

"Um, she's pretty busy. You know, we kind of grew apart. The Big Sister I had before that was busy, too." I couldn't believe it. This girl was a serial Little! One thing was certain. I wouldn't be leaving her. She needed me and I wasn't going to let her down.

I had planned an easygoing first outing, but with Terry breathing down my neck I figured I'd better up my game. It seemed doubtful that hanging out playing Pictionary (the only board game I currently owned) was going to cut it, so after grabbing a couple of disposable cameras, I drove us straight to the Santa Monica Pier, where I handed over fifteen dollars for parking. We rode the Ferris wheel, then the roller coaster, ate soft pretzels, and I even won her a stuffed iguana after about forty dollars' worth of tries at the Coke bottle ring toss. If there'd been a sound track under us, it would have been a perfect movie montage—especially because Ashley barely spoke the entire time. I felt myself working hard to forge a connection with her, but she answered any questions I asked with one-word responses and I'd usually have to ask the same question three times. It was like spending the day with

Marlee Matlin—only Marlee would've offered to pay for at least a soda. On the way home, I asked her if she had fun. "It was okay. Next time could we go to Magic Mountain?"

"I have an idea," I said, pulling into the parking lot of CVS. I wanted to get us a journal. It would be our Big Sister/Little Sister journal, and I figured we could paste photos we took together in it, color stuff, cut pictures out of magazines, and keep a record of all of our Big Sister/Little Sister outings. It would be a keepsake for her to look through later and remember that when the chips were down, she always had me in her life to lift her spirits and guide her way.

Okay, hold up, was Ashley eyeing a pack of Marlboros behind the counter? "This way, young lady." I steered her away from the smokes and toward the Hello Kitty notebooks, purchased some markers and glitter, and then took her home, where I pasted some pictures into the journal, sprinkled the glitter, added decorative stickers, and then wrote a little paragraph about our day. Meanwhile, Ashley and Patrice watched TV the whole time, completely oblivious to the fact that I was in the same room with them. Before leaving, I told Ashley she needed to call me anytime during the week so we could arrange another outing and that she should think of two ideas for things we could do together. The caseworker had told the Bigs to let our Littles be part of the process. It was up to them to help figure out activities.

Ashley never called me. But on Thursday Patrice did.

"Hello, Stefanie? This is Ashley's mom, Patrice. When are you picking her up?"

"Oh, hi, Patrice. I was hoping Ashley would call me herself, but how's Saturday?"

"Well, I'm going to be home on Saturday—I need you to take her when I've got to be somewhere else. Can you come on Sunday? I gotta get my hair done." I sincerely hoped Ashley's mom knew this wasn't a babysitting service.

"Okay, I can come on Sunday. Why don't I pick her up around noon?"

"Can you drop her off around six? I need to get it colored, too."

"I was actually thinking that a couple of hours would be plenty. Why don't I plan to have her back by three?" I thought I detected her sucking her teeth in disapproval, but I chose to ignore it.

On Sunday when I arrived to get Ashley, she got into the car looking irritated. "What are we going to do?"

"What would you *like* to do?"

"I don't know." I had assumed this would be the case given Ashley's winning personality, so I'd come up with an option.

"Okay, well, I thought we could go to my apartment and make pita pizzas and rent a movie. How does that sound?"

"I don't like pita pizza, whatever that is. I want to go out for Chinese food."

"Chinese food it is." I prayed that the Pick Up Sticks near my apartment ran their lunch specials on weekends.

We sat in silence over our orange chicken (full price). I tried to ask her all kinds of questions, but she gave her usual one-word answers or ignored me completely until we were done and I was settling up the bill.

"I want to go to the mall. I need some new lip gloss. Chanel." *You're nine, you ungrateful brat. You don't need lip gloss; you need a better attitude.*

"Do you have any money?" I asked.

"No. Don't you?"

"Um . . ." I was actually hoping the thirty-two dollars I charged to my Visa for the Chinese food wouldn't put me over my limit.

"We're not going to the mall. How about a walk in the park?"

"*Terry* always bought me lip gloss."

On our way back from the mall, I dropped Ashley off at her home, where she hopped out of the car with her new lip gloss and ran into her apartment. No "You're the greatest Big Sister ever!" No "I had fun." Not even "Thanks." At that point I would've been happy if she just waved.

Before pulling away, I reached into the Macy's bag for the lip gloss I'd bought for myself and it was gone. That little bitch stole my lip gloss! And Red Serenade wasn't even her color! I glanced down at the Big Sister literature I still had on my dashboard. *"Volunteering is fun! Being a Big Sister is simple and rewarding. It is as easy as showing your new Little Sister how to play a favorite computer game, bake an apple pie, or reading the funnies together. We've learned that being someone special to a child doesn't take much more than that. But the impact is huge—for both of you!"* Ha.

The next couple of outings went about the same way. I'd suggest the park or a game of ping-pong at the local rec center and she'd look at me like I'd grown a mustache. We'd end up at an arcade or movie—where she'd need her *own* large popcorn, candy, and drink. I didn't know how much longer I could keep this up—at this rate, I'd need a second job.

I didn't see Ashley for two weeks. I needed the time to save up my energy and money for our next outing. During that time, she never called me, but her mom did again and again, leaving me messages.

"Ashley really wants to see you. When are you going to take her out?" *Was that true?* I wondered. Maybe she did want to see me. I wasn't in the business of letting down nine-year-olds in need of my special brand of mentoring—even if they were kleptos. I figured hanging out with me was the only thing standing between her and juvie. And after all, it hadn't been that long ago that I'd saved a certain group of thirteen-year-olds from a life of prostitution.

A few days later, I called back, and although Ashley was too busy to come to the phone, Patrice was kind enough to arrange for me to come get her the following weekend. This time I was determined not to clear out my bank account trying to outdo Terry. I had a lot to offer. I'd always considered myself to be pretty good company—especially if you like snarky humor. I was determined to have a breakthrough with Ashley. When she got in the car, I told her we were going to Color Me Mine. She looked at me like I had just suggested we spend the day collecting aluminum cans. It's not like I actually wanted to go to Color Me Mine either; I had zero interest in painting a coaster shaped like a kitty cat or a miniature flower pot, but it seemed like an appropriate activity for a nine-year-old so I was sacrificing.

"I don't want to go to Color Me Mine. I want to go see *Like Mike*. Little Bow Wow's in it."

"Maybe next time. Today we're going to go express ourselves. You'll love it." She didn't speak the whole way there. I considered opening up a dialogue about how it's wrong to steal lip gloss out of your Big Sister's Macy's bag, but I didn't have the energy.

"I want to go home," Ashley muttered under her breath, like a pouty toddler.

"Me, too," I said.

"Are we at least going out to lunch first or are you going to let me starve?" I wondered what the Big Sisters Organization's policy was on bitch slapping nine-year-olds.

At Color Me Mine, I realized I'd made a huge mistake. I would have gotten off cheaper if we'd gone to Magic Mountain. Painting a single mug was fifteen bucks and that didn't include the charge for the kiln. Between the two of us, we weren't going to get out for less than forty bucks. To make matters worse, suddenly Ashley got into the gift-giving spirit.

"I want to make something for my mom's birthday. And my cousin's birthday's coming up, too. Actually, two cousins 'cause they're twins." An hour and a half and a hundred and thirty dollars later, we were finally on our way home. I couldn't wait to drop her off.

"That was boring," Ashley said. "Terry never made me do stupid stuff like that." Terry could have her.

When I got her home, her mother wasn't there. I had called ahead and left a message, and Patrice knew what time I was dropping her off, so this was confusing to me. I tried her cell again and again but got no response.

"You can go," Ashley said, letting herself into the apartment with her key.

"No. I can't," I said, following her inside, where she curled up on the couch hugging her knees to her chest and clicked on the TV. "I can't leave a nine-year-old girl home alone."

"My mom does it all the time." Damn. Suddenly I felt bad. Poor thing. No wonder she was such a little deviant. We sat on the couch together in silence until her mother finally pulled up an hour and a half later.

On my way home, I called my Big Sister/Little Sister caseworker. "I have some bad news," I said. "I won't be able to participate in the program any longer."

"That's really too bad. Ashley seems to go through a lot of Bigs."

"Yeah, well, I'm sorry but although I feel like I have a lot to offer, Ashley and I just aren't connecting. Maybe you can get Terry back. She seemed to really like her."

"Terry?"

"Yeah, her last Big?"

"We've never had anyone named Terry. In fact, her last Big Sister was named Jennifer and she only lasted one day."

Of course. Ashley had been toying with me all along. I was actually relieved. I wasn't a bad person. I was a giver. I was a thousand dollars in debt to prove it! I checked the coin compartment in my car and noticed it too had been cleaned out. Make that a thousand and two dollars.

"Would you be interested in being matched with another Little?" my caseworker asked, hopefully. *Not unless you give them a background check.* "The thing is, my schedule is really overbooked right now. But I'll call you if things loosen up." I hung up the phone, put my foot on the gas, and turned on the stereo. Screw this, I have a real live little sister. I mean, she's in her twenties and we have little to nothing in common, but at least she has her own bank account and is sharp enough to know that Red Serenade is not her color.

The Pirate Ship

After nine months of dating, my boyfriend, Jon, decided to put our relationship to the test with a trip to Mexico. We had spent three full seasons together with only mild squabbles, so naturally I had to see how this sucker would hold up under the dual pressures of travel and tequila. Now, nine months is a reasonably long time in my mind. A lot can happen in that span: cells the size of a sesame seed can blossom into a full-blown screaming infant; Pam Anderson can marry and divorce Tommy Lee, contract Hep C, marry Kid Rock, divorce Kid Rock, let Tommy Lee back in her life, and then break up with him again. And Sanjaya can have an entire career.

Some people say that opposites attract. I give anyone in a relationship who says that a year tops. Our choice in vacation destination was one of the many things I already loved about Jon. We shared a general disdain for the great outdoors.

Getting up at the crack of dawn and taking a brisk hike wearing shorts with fourteen pockets is something we'd both gladly pay to avoid. I haven't seen the inside of a sleeping bag since I was about twelve. Between the two of us, we own zero clothing items bearing the logo The North Face, and neither of us has ever owned a picnic basket or even understood the desire to use one. Why would anyone voluntarily pack up food, utensils, and napkins, and drag them all to another location to eat? We barely like the idea of eating in our backyard—it just seems like too much work for the few minutes of "Isn't this lovely? We're dining alfresco," immediately followed by "Fuck! I just got stung by a bee!" and then having to pick up all the stuff and move to the safe side of the screen door. Jon and I get along so well because we both believe that too much effort is overrated. I've never been attracted to those people who advertise themselves as loving "long walks on the beach." I love a beach, too, but you know what's better than a long walk on the beach? A short walk on the beach. Or better yet? Just sitting on a beach. And if I could sit on a beach and simultaneously watch TV, well, that would truly be living.

A beach in Mexico was the perfect plan for us. This wasn't a "get to know you trip"—we'd already spent the holidays together, been sick with the flu together, spent an entire day in bed watching a marathon of *Real World: Boston,* met each other's parents, and he'd even blown off an important deadline to see me through a particularly intense migraine attack—by bringing me three different choices of Starbucks coffee (caffeine helps), reheating a washcloth over and over in the bathroom sink to put on my head, and holding my hand all night. We were tight.

Everything on our trip thus far had been perfect in the way that vacations can only be nine months in, when you have nothing to do but sleep, have sex, lie on the beach (wearing SPF 80), and read. We stayed on a small private island an hour-long speedboat ride off the coast that boasted only eight casitas, which are basically little private houses. We ate seafood burritos and drank Coronas for breakfast, we dared each other to make a sex tape but backed out at the last minute, and we drank the most perfectly brewed Mexican coffee that it practically ruined us for store-bought brands. At night, all the residents of our little island joined together in the main house for gourmet eight-course meals. Every night we would drink red wine, divulge too much information about our private lives, and then head back to our casitas to fall asleep by nine. We were there for six perfect days and nights marred only by my accidentally saying something along the lines of, "I'm pretty sure I want to have children. Do you think we'll have children? Because I need to be with someone who is definitely at least interested in having children," mainly because I was premenstrual, thirty-three, and possibly having such a perfect time I felt the need to take a stab at sabotaging it in some way. You don't have to have ever read *The Rules* or even heard of it to know that you don't say things like that if it's not your intention to scare the shit out of someone. But Jon didn't even hop in a canoe and paddle away for some alone time. He just said, "Not right now. But eventually." I knew my future was with this man.

So, clearly, things were going as smoothly as that fifth shot of Patron as we marked the final day of the trek by sitting on the patio of a beachside restaurant trying to hoard margaritas like squirrels preparing for the long winter to come. Our tipsy-tourist profile made us perfect marks for every local vendor who angled in on our table as if we were on Sucker Radar, and after a couple hours our kitschy collection included a brightly colored woven blanket, a standing candle holder in the shape of the sun meant to bring good luck, various representations of the Virgin Guadeloupe, and about fourteen thousand Chiclets (it's so hard to say no to the under-five street-vendor set).

Each evening during the prior week, from all around Puerto Vallarta bay, we had seen a pirate ship edge across the horizon. It was an old-fashioned *Pirates of the Caribbean* knockoff, and I was obsessed with it. It was inevitable, then, that one of our orbiting flock of vendors would arrive with a notebook filled with glossy pictures of blissed-out couples on a sunset voyage aboard this magic vessel. He told us that for the special amigo rate of fifty bucks a head, we could embark on a four-hour dinner cruise featuring a dinner of filet mignon, unlimited drinks, a mariachi band, and—weather willing—a gorgeous sunset. I imagined our last night together on vacation standing on the deck of a huge ship, gazing into each other's eyes and clinking margarita glasses while being serenaded by the romantic beats of the mariachi band. It would be so dreamy! Maybe Jon would even propose!

After all, he'd pretty much agreed that we're having children. Because Jon wanted to please me (and because I was begging for it like a dog under the dinner table), he said, "It's our last night. Let's go on the pirate ship. Let's do it."

At about 5 p.m. we made our way to the pirate ship dock, having bullied an older Scottish couple into joining us. They'd been sitting at a nearby table drinking themselves into a receptive mood, and hearing us talk about it got them interested. So I convinced them it would be twice as fun with another couple, plus they were Scottish and the Scots are pretty reliable for being fun people to drink with. They like their booze as much as the Irish, but their accents are a touch more understandable. Standing on the dock an hour later with our new best friends, Fiona and Andrew, tanned, toasted, and in love, life felt full of promise.

After about four seconds aboard, it was clear we'd made a horrible mistake. The first clue? Our ship's crew was comprised of hyperenthusiastic pirate-attired little people. They were like little meth-mad Mexican sea bandits. If you can't imagine anything more disconcerting than fourteen Tattoos from *Fantasy Island* accosting you the second you board, try picturing them shirtless, sporting only bandannas and black and white MC Hammer pants. You're welcome.

Compounding our distress, the romantic seagoing restaurant from the glossy pictures was nowhere to be seen. In its place was a floating disco, sent across time and space from Queens, New York, circa 1979. Stacks of speakers were everywhere we looked, and a DJ perched on the bridge where

Blackbeard once had roamed. Also, about seventy percent of our fellow passengers were sun-scorched frat guys and their seminaked dates. I immediately suspected that our friendly vendor had two very different brochures selling the same cruise. The blaring of techno music at unbearable decibels kept us from having a reasoned discussion about fleeing back down the plank, so with the nervous hope that this was only the boarding spectacle, we lurched forward, waved on by our manic hosts.

"Señorita! Señor!" the midgets shrieked at us over the blaring music. "Drink, drink!" In fact, more booze was actually a great idea given the situation unfolding. Unfortunately, what they were offering was a sickly sweet grain alcohol punch just like the swill that had laid me out cold once when I drank it out of a bathtub at a high school party at fifteen. I choked down about half a plastic cup before I tossed it overboard, where I'm sure it eventually killed a seagull. Jon and I made a beeline for the farthest place from any sort of speakers or little people in big pants to stand but there was really nowhere to hide. What had looked so massive and peaceful floating along the ocean while we were sipping margaritas on the shore now seemed smaller than a New York City apartment bathroom. And there were three hours and fifty-nine minutes left to go.

Within moments of setting sail, the DJ bellowed that it was time for the traditional flag raising ceremony, which was "just for the beautiful ladies." I tried to make myself look as unattractive as possible, but apparently by beautiful ladies they meant anyone in possession of a vagina. One of the grinning Tattoos literally dragged me away from Jon in spite of my protests. I had him by at least a foot and a half, but the little man was a master of leverage, and I was quickly whisked to the bow to join the rest of the "beautiful ladies." We were forced to hold hands and dance in circles around the entire deck of the boat while the men stood above us hooting and hollering. It was worse than a construction site. When I knew I couldn't take one more moment of this, I tried to find Jon in the crowd to catch his eye, and make him see that he must save me. I finally spotted him in the crowd and I thought I saw him smiling, although it was hard to tell for sure because he was busy videotaping the entire debacle. That's when I started to get mad.

By the time I reached the rear deck, I knew Jon didn't share my pain. We both stood along the raised stern, where I tried in vain to block out the line dancing, sombrero tossing, or vomiting over the side of the boat that was happening on the main floor. All the while Jon continued calmly videotaping instead of joining my profanity-filled rant. Our Scottish friends, having been forcibly separated during the flag raising, spotted us and reapproached. But faced with what they swiftly diagnosed as an ugly fight brewing between the Americans, they'd discreetly edged away, never to return.

By the time the DJ broke out the Macarena, I was on the verge of tears. I thought the Macarena had been outlawed a few years back, but apparently Mexican laws are different. The music got louder and louder. I prayed that cochlear implants would be covered by my insurance because they were definitely in my future. Jon, still glued to his viewfinder, didn't even make eye contact with me. He was clearly unfazed by the sonic, cultural, and emotional traumas being inflicted on the innocent. That's the moment I started to hate him.

With my buzz from earlier in the day having worn off in the absence of liquor that would willingly be consumed by adults, I was now facing this crisis without even the slightest buffer to the senses. Finally it was dinnertime and we were given a reprieve from the blaring disco and herded below decks, where our meal and one complimentary glass of reddish wine awaited.

"I have a bad feeling this wine was purchased at a 99-cents store and is actually not wine but furniture polish," I carped, hoping at last to draw him into my web of agony.

"You think?" Jon answered, sort of . . .

"Well, I can't read Spanish so I can't call them on it." Jon ignored me and drank his glass and mine, too.

"What?" I asked. As in *What's wrong? Besides this fucking cruise? Are you mad at me? Am I bugging you?* It was all in there. All in my single "What?"

"Nothing."

Immediately after I'd taken my last bite of filet mingoat, we were shooed back upstairs, where more activities awaited—two hours and fifty-three minutes' worth, by my watch, assuming we weren't fighting a headwind. Jon and I tried to sneak to an empty part of the boat but were immediately told that that area was off-limits and herded back toward the main deck, where game time was about to commence. The first game involved a woman who was called up to a makeshift stage and told to repeat a phrase into a microphone only . . . wait for it . . . she had an ice cube in her mouth so she couldn't say it correctly! And somehow it was supposed to be sexual, like she was attempting to give a blow job. Ha!

A sinister vibe seemed to take over around this time—similar to how I imagine the air felt right before the woman got gang-raped in Big Dan's Tavern. The frat boys were all riled up and circled around a woman onstage who was so drunk she was starting to turn the ice eating into an opportunity to do a striptease, taking the cube out of her mouth and rubbing it on her nipples as it melted. A nearby Tattoo helpfully tossed her more ice, because on the pirate ship the customer is king.

At that moment, our galleon of horrors began to creak. "Great, we're sinking!" I hissed. On second thought, I realized that a speedy trip to shore courtesy of the Mexican Coast Guard would be like having my sentence commuted by the governor.

"Relax, we're just coming about," said Jon.

"Huh?"

"It means we're turning around." Great, he was so comfortable with all of this that he was dropping nautical terms on me. I fought the urge to push him overboard. The worst part of this "coming about" meant that we were only at the halfway point. Two hours remained. I knew then that I'd have to make peace with the paint thinner they were pushing as punch if I was to survive till shore. I grabbed two red cups from the nearest Tattoo, held my nose, and tried to medicate.

How could Jon not see how horrible this was? What was the point of videotaping this fucking nightmare? Had he drunk the booze cruise Kool-Aid? Could he be enjoying himself? I was completely alone in this. If he was having a horrible time couldn't he just yell, "This is horrible!" just once? He had totally withdrawn, burying his head not in the sand but behind the camera, ignoring me. I'd been wrong about him. We were nothing alike.

Then when it didn't seem like it could get any worse, the DJ stopped the music and directed our attention to the makeshift stage below him for a special treat. Two Tattoos entered with a pair of roosters with things that looked like spurs attached to their claws. It was a cock fight. This just couldn't be happening. Who ever heard of a sunset, mariachi band, filet mignon cruise with a cock fight?

That's when all hell broke loose. Two drunk sorority girls started crying and their boyfriends put their arms around them to shield them from the cruelty while secretly stealing glances at the potential carnage.

I couldn't take any more and yelled at Jon's video camera, "What the fuck? What's wrong with you? Two birds are going to fight to the death and you are fucking videotaping it?" Jon finally lowered the video camera and looked at me like he just found a filled prescription for lithium in my medicine cabinet. Through gritted teeth he said, "Listen, I don't want to be here any more than you do but, unless we swim for shore, we're stuck here. What exactly do you want me to do about it? *Jesus!*"

What I wanted him to do about it was run up on stage and either set the birds free, or kill them humanely and then roast them to make up for the horrendous dinner; I wanted him to take me in his arms and say, *"Baby, right now this feels like the worst thing that's ever happened to us. We made a horrible mistake and I can't wait to get off this Godforsaken hell cruise just as much as you! And the second we hit land and get back home we will laugh about this, but in the meantime, let's just try to get through it. Together. I love you. Marry me."* Instead, he completely ignored me. So I broke up with him right then and there in my head. I was halfway back to drunk and furious. I mentally packed my bags to move out of his apartment despite the fact that we didn't exactly live together. Once we got back to his place, I'd get my toothbrush, the couple pairs of underwear I kept in a drawer, my scrunchy, oh, and the Pyrex dish I left there from when I made him a turkey lasagna. He was going to miss me. Was another girl going to make him turkey lasagna? Doubtful.

We didn't speak for the remainder of the cruise or in the cab on the way back to our hotel. Screw him, I thought as we lie in separate beds in the hotel room, still not speaking. I cried softly. I would be fine. I had friends. I had a great life! I had work, plus my friends would make me margaritas and tell me what an asshole they always thought he was. It would be just like *Sex and the City*, minus Charlotte because I didn't have any friends that boring. But I'd be great. Single but great! I couldn't wait to get back into the swing of things.

"Come on. Get over here," Jon growled from his bed, extending his hand out like a bridge back to dry land. There was no time for pride. In one second, I was wrapped up in his arms, which still smelled ever so slightly of the ocean, and just before we fell asleep he whispered gently in my ear, "ARRRRR."

Marry Me, Dumbass

The morning after Jon asked me to marry him, three and a half years into our relationship, he woke up with ugly black bruises all over his upper arms. As it turned out, those bruises were the result of me punching him repeatedly in an effort to pummel him into proposing. In my defense, I had *a lot* of Pinot Grigio in me, and he kept taunting me, snarling, "It doesn't hurt . . . Is that all you got? I couldn't even feel that one. Wait, did an animated fairy just tap my arm?"

I had been dating Jon for just over two years when I started a full frontal assault to get him to marry me. I broke all the rules that have ever been written to help women like me, women with no impulse control, women with no shame, women who need a clearer understanding of the line between expressing affection and stalking. The rules I'm speaking of are anything uttered by Dr. Laura, any article ever published in *Cosmopolitan* that doesn't involve an orgasm, and mainly the ones in the book *The Rules* (written by two women, one of whom is now divorced). On closer review, I'd been rule breaking with wild abandon since we had started dating:

Never Accept a Weekend Date Later Than Wednesday. Check. What was I supposed to do, pretend to consult with my imaginary day runner that keeps track of my many phantom appointments to see if I had other prior engagements with my many nonexistent suitors?

Don't Call Him and Rarely Return His Calls. This one makes no sense—especially since it was written before texting became our primary means of communication. Now you can text back and forth while having minor surgery under local anesthetic. In fact, I wouldn't be surprised if people text while *performing* minor surgery. So, back in the primitive days of landlines, if you played that hard to get how were you supposed to make plans? Morse code, smoke signals, homing pigeons, cave etchings?

Don't Open Up Too Fast. This one is far too nebulous and open for interpretation. Sure, announcing you've had five abortions in the last three years is probably information best saved until you've at least met his parents (preferably not *during* that meeting, unless conversation gets slow), but for me, a first date is boring unless I get to hear and tell at least one Crazy Ex story.

Don't See Him More Than Once or Twice a Week. This is probably great advice, even though I didn't follow it. I get it: seem in high demand to add to your allure. But while I was spending so much time with Jon going for sushi, sneaking into movies, having great sex, and falling in love, all I really missed were TV shows. On second thought, what was I thinking? This was pre TiVo. To this day I have no idea how things wound up between Dharma and Greg. So, okay, point taken.

Always End the Date First. "I'm having a fabulous time but, darn it, I almost forgot I have an 11 p.m. eyebrow and upper lip wax appointment so I'm gonna have to cut this short" is a perfect way to really retain an air of mystery . . . or make someone suspect you may have Borderline Personality Disorder.

Don't Talk Too Much. Really? Have these people ever met a woman? I could have my jaw wired shut and I'd still find a way to monopolize a conversation. I think the authors should amend that rule to *Don't Talk Too Much About Boring Shit* 'cause sure, no one wants to be subjected to a four-hour soliloquy on your sister-in-law's recovery from a wisdom tooth extraction, but in general, I'm a fan of talking.

Don't Rush into Sex. Finally, one rule I didn't break. In spite of Jon's murmured claims to the contrary, I waited six dates to do the deed with him, which, these days, I think even a nun would be high-fiving me.

But once Jon and I moved in together without being engaged (yes, I know, another huge rule shattered to bits), my rule breaking took on a new ferocity. Having once lived with someone before that didn't end happily, I let Jon know under *no uncertain terms* that I would not be moving in with him unless we were at least engaged.

"But I've never lived with anyone before." He whined like he was still in his college dorm instead of in his mid thirties living alone in an apartment. I should stipulate that it was an apartment with at least twenty dusty baseball hats lined across his curtain rod, a sure sign of maturity. If that wasn't enough of a clue, there was always the lamp made out of a wine jug on the nightstand next to his bed. At that point, why not just walk around with a hat made entirely out of Budweiser cans? Really get the message out there as to where you are emotionally.

"That lamp was a gift from my sister! She made it!" he snapped defensively when I innocently pointed it out. Hey, my mother once got me a pair of Indian-style feather earrings that were all the rage *never,* but they "made her think of me" when she saw them. That didn't mean I had to wear them.

"Well, I *have* lived with someone and you know how

that turned out, so I want to be absolutely sure where you're headed with this," I said, digging in.

"I just never saw myself getting married without living with the person first. That's just how it's done. I don't want to miss a step." Miss a step? *We're not putting together a desk from Ikea. There are no step-by-step instructions. We're in love, asshole!*

"Okay, but you're moving in with me because at this point you plan to marry me right?"

"Yeah."

"Well, okay then. As long as we're clear." What the hell was I talking about? Clear on what? He wasn't promising anything. He was just saying that yeah, at some point in the future, possibly after I reached menopause, or maybe after I'd been in a tragic accident, fallen into a coma, and he sat by my bedside playing me John Mayer songs and reading me articles from *The Onion* trying to bring me back to consciousness, he would realize he was ready to tie the knot. I didn't have that kind of time; that could take months. I needed a better plan.

Living together was actually pretty great. Being with Jon day in and day out, grocery shopping together, and making my own special dent in his couch had only deepened my feelings for him. And with the new level of commitment, I calmed down quite a bit. I rarely even *thought* about needing to get married. Sure, I made the occasional remark every other week or so—just a little nudge to make sure we were moving in the right direction.

"So, you don't feel like there's something you need to get out of your system before you get married, right?" I asked one day over our morning coffee.

"Like what?" he asked.

"I don't know, like hiking through the Himalayas or backpacking through Europe—staying at youth hostels the whole way or banging a Czech model?"

"Nope. I'm good. I'm not like Emmett." Emmett was Jon's best friend who Jon swore would have to sell a screenplay before he committed to any woman.

"Okay, cool. So there are no real holdups. Good to know."

"Nope," he said, popping a piece of toast in the toaster— a toaster that I had brought with me when I moved in. Yeah, if it hadn't been for me, he would've just been eating plain-old cold wheat bread. There'd be no delicious warm crust for the butter to melt on. Just dumb, stupid, uninteresting *non*toasted bread! Could it be any clearer what I was bringing to the table here? *How could he not see that we needed to be married!*

And this is how we went along for a while until Emmett, who'd known his girlfriend, Sarah, for all of six months, called up one night and told Jon he was engaged. When Jon gave me the news, I was less than thrilled. I really liked Emmett's girlfriend; in fact, I'd made out with her one night after we all drank way too much Cabernet and the boys promised us La Perla lingerie (which we never got) if we kissed with tongue. And I figured they'd get married eventually, but I didn't think it would be before us.

"Really? Which studio bought his screenplay?" I asked, trying to keep any sign of pissiness out of my voice.

There's no reasonable explanation for why I wanted to be engaged so badly. I know many couples who are perfectly happy living together forever, people who believe that marriage is "just a piece of paper" and that if two people are meant to be together they will stay together and if they're not meant to be, the mere act of saying vows won't change that. There are people who feel secure and happy just living "in the now." I'm not one of those people. And I have a strong feeling those people smoke a lot of dope.

I started picking up steam in the No Shame department. In fact, one night, I proposed to him in our carport after a night out with Emmett and Sarah. "Jon," I purred. "I think we should get married. I want you to be my family. I want to be able to visit you in the hospital if you're sick, you know, be your next of kin and all of that, the whole package. I want to have your last name. So marry me. Just say you'll marry me and then we'll be engaged. Look, you can always divorce me if it doesn't work out. It's not like getting a tattoo. And hey, we could have a double ceremony with Emmett and Sarah!"

"I do want to marry you. But I want to ask, when I'm ready."

"Okay, so can I take that as a yes?"

It's not that a woman shouldn't propose to a man; in fact, I've seen it done successfully. But it's probably not exactly attractive to see a woman *beg* a man to marry her, especially when said man has made it clear that he is on his own course, which is more difficult to chart than storm systems, tides, or weather. I'm not a meteorologist.

The problem was, I was in a hurry to marry him and he . . . was in no huge hurry to do anything. The man spent the better part of two years buying a car. He'd been driving a Honda Prelude that had more mileage on it than Jenna Jameson but with none of the cosmetic upkeep. Seriously, two years narrowing down his options, checking and rechecking *Consumer Reports,* test driving, negotiating, talking it over with friends, getting close to a decision, but then second guessing. At one point, he finally decided on an Audi, negotiated his best deal, and then took so long to pull the trigger, someone else bought it out from under him. Eventually, he committed to a three-year lease on an Acura. This was not a guy to choose a bride in a timely manner. And in spite of having always seen myself as independent and a bit free-spirited, I had set my sights on spending the rest of my life with this guy and didn't want to end up as that Audi. But much like a car dealer, I couldn't fathom why it was taking him so long to sign the pink slip. In fact, it was starting to piss me off. What was the holdup? He was thirty-five when I met him and now he was thirty-seven. Did he think he was going to meet someone else better? Because I, for one, knew I wasn't going to meet anyone half as great as Jon.

This was not a matter of just wanting to be married; in fact, there was a big part of me that before meeting Jon never wanted to get married at all. I was never that teenager who got a tingly feeling down there from pawing through bridal magazines with sweaty hands, dreaming about my wedding to Scott Baio, trying to decide if I'd be going with an updo or if I was more of a long hair with flowers type of bride. Even now, I wouldn't know which fork to eat salad with unless one had a little picture of a salad on it to help me out.

I wanted to marry Jon. I wanted to marry him because I honestly couldn't see myself waking up next to anyone else besides him ever again. I wanted to marry him because every day he lost his keys and every day I knew exactly where they were; because he always brought me a bottle of water to put by my bedside at night; because he'd never, ever used an emoticon in any email; because he wanted to stab the character Aiden from *Sex and the City* through the throat; because I'd never met a sweeter smart-ass; because he'd never, *ever* been inside a Color Me Mine do-it-yourself pottery store. I wanted to marry him because he didn't have potential; he was perfect. And . . . okay, maybe I wanted to marry him so I could be on his health insurance, but . . . still . . . I'd kissed enough addicts, new age enthusiasts, men who thought yoga retreats were a great idea, men who believed the homeless problem could be solved if they'd all just "go get a job," and men who wore overalls to know better.

So I made a decision: I wasn't going to be issuing any ultimatums. Maybe that made me some kind of sucker, but I didn't care. I refused to be one of "those girls"—the ones who couldn't wait to be engaged so that they could run up to other women who were engaged and scream, "Ooooh, myyyy Gawd! Look at my ring! It's *huge*!" I wanted to be with Jon more than I wanted to be married. I knew for a fact that if I gave him an ultimatum, and he didn't propose to me, I wasn't going anywhere. He was stuck with me. Soon after, his perpetually single friend Jack (who had such bad luck with women that his last girlfriend could only climax if she got punched in the stomach) finally met the love of his life and within months promptly proposed. I was unfazed, even when Jon flew to Vegas for the bachelor party and got lap dances from strippers—one in particular whom he swears to this day only got his repeat business because she was giving him great real estate advice. Meanwhile, I was sentenced to the boring-ass bridal shower, where we played "guess who knows Marley the best?" After four brief meetings, here's a guess: *not me*. There are very few get-togethers I hate more than bridal showers. But women seem to love 'em. These ladies were so excited by the cake, I could've been in the corner giving myself a breast exam and no one would've noticed. So, I ate a ton of guacamole, drank a mimosa, and hit the road, barely, I mean *barely* at all, tearing up to a George Strait song on the twenty-five-mile lonely ride home. But seriously, I was fine. *I didn't need to be married.*

A few months later, we went to a Super Bowl party at the home of the happily newlywed couple, Emmett and Sarah. We were just hanging out eating turkey pepperoni, gouda cheese and crackers, drinking wine, and having a great time until our friend Gigi, who'd been with her boyfriend, Kurt, for . . . well, who the hell knows, but the point is, suddenly, in slow motion, she raised her left hand and said, "I have an announcement" all girlie, and all I thought was *she better not be getting married because then I really will be the last of our group to get married. Plus, she's way too cool for that. She's a guy's girl! She loves football, she's a teacher, a feminist . . .*

"Kurt and I are engaged!"

I practically choked on my Ritz. I could barely smile. "That's so great! I've got to grab something from the kitchen," I said. I left the room and lost it behind the freezer. Sarah was sent for. At that point, I hoped the rest of the guests thought I had my period and needed a tampon—even that would've been less embarrassing than crying over the fact that my stupid boyfriend wouldn't propose. Sarah did her best to console me.

"He's going to marry you, Stef. I know he is. I don't know what he's waiting for, but I know he is going to marry you. You know how he is; it takes him forever to make a decision about which color Converse sneakers to buy."

"I know," I sobbed. "I promised myself I wouldn't do this anymore. I'm mortified and I feel pathetic. Don't tell Gigi." Sure, being able to make any situation about myself was a talent but sometimes a talent that's best kept hidden.

Later that night, I drank a little too much wine and got right back to shaming myself in earnest. "When are you going to propose? You said you were going to. You said you wanted to marry me and it's been over three years! If you're not going to marry me, just tell me now so I can get used to that fact and not keep hoping for something that will never happen." I got no real response. So I took the hint and waited a couple of weeks . . . fine, *two days* before trying again. But first I cooked him a great dinner and drank a couple of glasses of wine. And then I started asking again. And a few nights later, the same thing. And then a couple of nights later, the same thing, except that this night it got violent. This is where I started playfully punching him in the arms. Then not so playfully, then he started egging me on. All of a sudden, he got aggravated and said, "Do you really want to ruin the surprise?"

"Surprise?"

"Yes, dumbshit, the surprise."

"I'd very much like to ruin the surprise. I don't want to be surprised. I want to be engaged." And with that, for some reason, I stomped off to our bedroom and lie on the bed, possibly to watch the room spin around or maybe to watch *Six Feet Under* and feel sorry for myself. I heard a rustling in the kitchen and then Jon came into the bedroom with two handmade Color Me Mine mugs, which he placed down next to me on the bed. *Oh my God, the man had gone to Color Me Mine. If that's not true love, I don't know what is.*

The first one said, "Happy Anniversary to My Bitch." Our three-year dating anniversary had passed six months before, so I had no idea where he was going with this. Then I saw the other mug: "Wanna Get Hitched?"

"I tried to give you these six months ago. I left them in front of the coffeemaker, but you refused to go get me coffee. You had just started at work and you had some meeting you had to get to."

"Well, why didn't you try again the next day then?"

"I did. But you rushed out the door again."

"And there were no other days available in your schedule for proposing?"

"Well, time kind of got away from me, and then it seemed ridiculous to give you the mugs since it was no longer close to our anniversary. So I figured I'd come up with something else."

"And it's six months later and you still haven't come up with anything else?"

"Well, no. I was working on it."

"Okay, then. My answer is yes. I would love to marry you!" And then I called everyone I knew to say, "Ooooh, myyyy Gawd! Guess what?!"

Zorro!

It was one of those typical days where the only way I made it to the gym was by bribing myself with the promise of getting something pretty afterward, like a sparkly new lip gloss or a Croissan'Wich—a bargain at only 29 grams of fat. Although I live in Los Angeles, where I have been known to shop at Whole Foods and throw down a hundred bucks for artichoke chicken garlic sausages, a cube of tofu, and some Burt's Bees hand lotion, I still maintain a cheapo membership to a national chain gym. It's a pretty low-rent operation despite its claims of quality and the dozens of classes available to its members—well, except for any class that involves an activity popularized in this decade, like boxing, hip-hop, Pilates, or yoga. No, those are extra. The basic membership classes are followed by descriptions like "low impact," "light toning," or "only slight chance of hip breakage." The median age in these classes is about seventy-six, and at least half the attendees still think matching headbands and leg warmers are a sweet idea. And yes, that includes the men. It's like one minute you're in Hollywood and the next minute you're in 1986.

Luckily, I don't care about classes anyway, since I have no interest in jumping around to bad disco music, forcing me to pretend I threw my back out so I can protect my dignity when I bolt out early and go get a prescription for muscle relaxants. Plus the fact that the classes invite socializing, and for me, chatting it up with other people while I'm wearing little more than a sports bra does not equal a good time.

Although I'd gotten it together enough to get in the car and drive there, I was feeling especially lazy. Sure, I was there for a workout, but I still drove around the parking lot for a half hour trying to find the very closest spot to the front door to save myself any unnecessary exertion. But, because I'd put off my workout until the busiest time of day, I ended up parking all the way near the back of the lot and I couldn't help but get irritated thinking about how thoughtless it was of my gym not to provide some sort of shuttle service. Note to self: Drop a note into the suggestion box if they have one.

When I got out on the floor, I realized there were lines for all the treadmills, elliptical machines, and Stairmasters— there were even lines for the scales, which was bewildering: What kind of masochists would willingly subject themselves to the spectacle of a public weigh-in? I would rather repeat junior high than weigh myself in the middle of a crowded gym fully dressed. Personally, I only like to weigh myself first thing in the morning, completely naked on an empty bladder. I've been known to tweeze my brows before stepping on a scale but, then again, it's been well established that I have issues. So, due to the crowd, I was forced to stand around reading my *National Enquirer*—which, FYI, I only buy for the crossword puzzle—while I waited for a Precor machine.

Eventually I got a seat at the chest machine that always makes me think of *Are You There God? It's Me Margaret*—so much so that I can't help but chant ever so softly under my breath, "We must, we must, we must increase our bust." It was there that I first heard *the Sound:* a groaning, guttural grunt like someone having great sex or a grand mal seizure. It seemed to be coming from behind me somewhere, but it was hard to tell exactly. The Sound was so loud it managed to pierce through the Kanye West blaring through my iPod ear buds. My head snapped around, expecting to see either a porno being shot or a situation that would require me to call paramedics. At first, I couldn't find the origin of the noise, but, finally, I spotted a woman in the back of the room working out with a personal trainer, who couldn't decide whether he was Zorro or the Latin version of Fabio. He had a black bandanna wrapped around his head pirate style, a black tank top that seemed purposely four sizes too small, and he was wearing a cape, seriously. At least that's how I remember it. Sure, I guess it's possible that under hypnosis I might hazily recall that it was only a black towel draped around his shoulders making me think of a cape. But until that happens, I stand by my cape memory.

With each lift of what looked like a two-pound hand

weight, the woman being trained by Zorro let loose with the Sound. I couldn't figure out why all the overexertion was happening; she wasn't in kick-ass shape but she wasn't completely out of shape either—more like someone who'd been hitting the soy sauce too hard for a few months. I attempted to ignore the whole scene and put my Kanye back on.

"Now I ain't sayin' she a gold digger (When I'm in need)
But she ain't messin' wit no broke niggas"

"Uuuuuuuuuuuuuuoooooooohhhhhyaaaaaaaaaaaaaaaa!!!!!" I clearly heard over the music.

"Get down girl, go 'head get down (I gotta leave)"

"OOOOOOOOOOOOOOOOOOOmmmmmmmmm aaaaaaaaaaaaaah"

What the hell? I ripped my ear buds out again—hearing someone get sodomized turns out to be more distracting than one would think. In fact, I'm surprised that so many people have been able to churn out novels while incarcerated.

"UUUUUUUHHHHRRRRRR*AAAAAAAAAAAAA HHHHUHHHHGGGGG"*

It was getting worse. So mid-set, I made a huge production of gathering my *Enquirer*, water bottle, and iPod and noisily stalked across the weight room to the sit-up station, hoping that my irritation was noticeable. But the *Sound* followed me. Even from a distance I could still hear her loud and clear. In fact, at this point, it was *all* I could hear. The Sound consumed all the air in the room. Sit up, Sound! Sit up, Sound. Rest. Sound. Since it was impossible to work out, I caught the eye of the woman on the crunch machine next to me and shook my head at her as a show of solidarity against the freaks at the gym.

In a way, I was not even surprised this was happening. Whenever I work out, I seem to have some sort of bad gym juju. There always seems to be some random dude karate chopping his way around the room, or a woman in a crowded class doing her own workout routine in the mirror, or a stark naked woman curling her hair in the locker room. Sure, those people are distracting, but at least they're quiet.

Just then, Zorro swaggered by for a drink of water. As he passed, he saw me staring at him in what I'm sure he mistook for a "God, I love a man in a cape" way, and with a vulgar smile he said, "How are you doing?" *How am I doing? How did he think I was doing? I was livid.*

I so badly wanted to say, "*How about getting that chick to tone down the Meg Ryan orgasm impressions so I could get in one more set of sit-ups in peace?*" but I was scared he might pull out the sword hanging down from his waist and challenge me to a duel. At least, I *hoped* it was a sword, but I wasn't taking any chances. So instead I opted for, "Is there any way you could ask the woman you're training to keep it down a little?" Zorro cocked his head like he was listening for banditos scaling the outside wall and headed back to the Sound.

Next thing I know, the Sound was in my face startling me

so badly I almost fell off the rowing machine I'd just barely figured out how to use. "Did you tell my trainer to tell me to be quiet?" she practically screamed in a Spanish accent that tends to sound passionate even if the person is just helping you with directions. *Wow, if I got into a fistfight in the gym at almost forty years old that would make a great story.* But then I also thought, *I am very opinionated and oftentimes, many of which when I've forgotten to take a Xanax, I can't keep my thoughts completely to myself and this behavior has led to no good in the past.* So I calmly said, "Your deafening workout noises are driving everyone nuts. Plus, there's a rule that says no loud or strange noises." I pointed to one of only about a hundred signs in the gym posting the rules, which people routinely ignore. Some of the rules include:

- No loud or strange noises that may distract other members
- Always use a workout towel
- Be courteous of others
- Limit cardio machine use to 30 minutes

And here's my brief wish list for more rules that shouldn't need to be posted but yet they seem to be necessary:

- Your workout towel is not for decoration
- Deodorant isn't optional
- If I can see the outline of your penis, your pants are too tight

- Cell phone talkers will be subject to nasty looks
- The basket on the Lifecycle bikes is not an empty Red Bull receptacle
- There's a reason you're wearing headphones; singing over them defeats the purpose

Without even a cursory glance at the rule I'd kindly pointed out, the Sound snapped back loudly, "I am paying eighty dollars an hour for a personal trainer so I'm entitled to be as loud as I want," which, obviously, makes no sense whatsoever. I started to get really pissed, not just for me but for everyone at the gym who has been bullied by this noise-polluting lunatic. So, since it seemed that no one else was going to stand up to her, feeling very much like Norma Rae, I screamed, "We are *all* members of this gym with equal rights regardless of whether or not we pay some stupid Zorro impersonator, in a stupid cape, to train us, and that entitles all of us to work out without having to listen to your fake orgasms. So either join another gym or shut the hell up and work out like a normal person." I'm not going to lie; I did sort of half expect the place to erupt in applause or perhaps participate in a quick round of "For She's a Jolly Good Fellow" but no one even made eye contact with me. Most people seemed to pretend I wasn't even there. Well, maybe *pretend* is too strong a word, but still, even a nod in my direction would have been appreciated.

The Sound responded by calling me something in Spanish that I couldn't understand, but I had a feeling if we were in Spain those would be fighting words, then said in English that she'd be waiting for me in the parking lot and stomped off. What was this, junior high?

I figured the best course of action seeing as we were both mature adults would be to tell on her. I was too shaken to continue any kind of workout anyway, and luckily I was pretty much done—more than two sets of stomach crunches is just overkill in my book and I'm morally opposed to stretching after exercise. I can understand stretching *before* you exercise, but that seems like more than enough. Why all the obsession with flexibility?

On my way to the women's locker room, I popped my head into the glass-enclosed offices of "management."

"Are you looking to join?" a young guy who couldn't have been older than fifteen in a polo shirt and ponytail asked way too eagerly.

"I'm already a member here. A paying member, and I'd like to lodge a formal complaint. Who do I need to speak to?"

"Well, I could help you but I'm about to give a tour right now. Maybe when I get back?"

"Isn't there someone else who could help me?"

"Um, Tim is in the next office but he's with the new trainees right now. You could come back in a half hour. But your best bet is to put it in the suggestion box." This was useless.

As I was turning the combination lock with shaking hands to get my stuff out of my locker, I spotted the girl I'd made eye contact with earlier doing sit-ups. When she saw me, she turned away almost as if she was trying to avoid me.

Impossible. I walked right up to her and said, "That was pretty insane, am I right? I mean, didn't it sound like she was having sex? Who could work out with that shit going on!" She looked at me a little fearfully, which I could completely understand—after all, we'd all been put through a traumatic experience—and slowly backed out of the locker room saying, "Yeah, there are some crazy people at this gym."

Exactly. Finally, someone else got it. I felt so much better; I grabbed a suggestion card from the box on my way out. Maybe I *would* lodge that complaint. And maybe I'd suggest the shuttle while I was at it. I figured I had some time because I'd need to wait for ponytail guy to get back from his tour to see if he could escort me to my car.

Deliverance

November 26, 2007

Besides the fact that I almost had a stroke when I found out I was pregnant with twins, the first half of my most recent and final pregnancy was fairly uneventful except for an unstoppable craving for bananas—I was buying bananas like a monkey with an allowance. "You must just need the potassium," a well-meaning nonparent friend once said as I hoovered my eighth banana of the morning.

"How much potassium is too much?" I asked. "Can you OD on potassium?"

"I don't think so. I once ate ten bananas when I was really, really high because I heard it helps you come down," my friend told me. Clearly, this was a question for someone with a medical degree, not just a girl with a prescription for medical marijuana due to cramps.

About twenty-eight weeks into my pregnancy, I went to my high-risk doctor for my latest of countless ultrasounds—which, by the way, I never took home in the form of a DVD, much to the surprise of the technicians. What was I going to do with it? Pull it out at parties and say, "Gather 'round, folks, time to watch some weird gray forms floating around on the screen that could be *Braveheart* or midget porn for all you can actually make out. But this ultrasound was different. First, the technician checked all the major anatomy, while I lie there asking what I thought were pertinent questions, such as, "Do you see a modeling career in their future? And if so, since they're not identical is there one whose career we should be focused on more?" But the tech had some disturbing news. One of the girls was quite a bit smaller than the other one. Like half the size. She couldn't discuss with me what that meant, so I had to lie there on the table and wait for the doctor to come in and explain what was going on. I really wish I hadn't picked that appointment to tell Jon I didn't need an escort.

Leaving me alone in a room with nothing but my thoughts is never a great idea—which is one of the many reasons I'm vehemently opposed to meditating—but it's an especially bad idea when I've been without Zoloft or alcohol in my system for almost seven months. The doctor waltzed in a solid forty-five minutes later in a great mood. I could swear he was whistling "Zip-a-Dee-Doo-Dah" and there may have been an animated bird singing on his shoulder. I was in a full-blown panic attack already at that point. "Why, hellooooo," Uncle Remus greeted me.

"So one of my babies is only a pound," I said, failing to keep the rising panic out of my voice. "That sounds bad."

At this point, despite my fear that parenting twins would loosen my already tenuous grip on sanity, I had grown quite attached to both my unborn daughters and the idea that something could be wrong was terrifying.

"Hey, now. Calm down there. There's really no way to know what this means, if anything, right now. It just depends on how they continue to grow."

"But at my stage of pregnancy it's not normal for one of the babies to be this little, right?"

"Perhaps Baby B is going to be naturally small." You have to respect doctors for their vagueness. I mean, sure, part of it is simply a God-given gift but it has to be exercised, like a muscle. The word "absolutely" has no place in a doctor's vocabulary. The only words that are used with any frequency are "perhaps," "possibly," "potentially," "depends," and "what kind of insurance do you have?"

I was given the advice to lie on my side for four hours a day to increase the flow of oxygen to Baby B, and the doctor would see me again in three weeks. *Three weeks?* That seemed way too long to wait if something was wrong. "And I should probably eat a lot more too, right?" I asked, hoping against hope that corned beef on rye was going to be part of my prescription.

"No. This has nothing to do with what you're eating or not eating. Your weight gain is fine." I did detect a slight "you're fat" vibe in his "your weight is fine" but I decided to be the bigger person and ignore it. I also decided to eat *a lot* more just to err on the safe side—McDonald's chocolate shakes made perfect sense since I heard somewhere that that's what Renée Zellweger did to gain weight to play Bridget Jones. If that was good enough for her, it would be fantastic for Baby B, whom I named Sadie. Since Jon and I had already chosen the name for one of the girls, I decided to give it to Baby B because I found out Sadie means "mercy" in Spanish. Turns out Sadie also means "princess" in Hebrew and happens to be a very popular name for a cat, but I chose to focus on the "mercy" part.

Everyone loves an obviously pregnant woman, so during those next three weeks it was a common occurrence for women to stop me on the street or in the grocery store or in the ladies' room and comment on my belly. "How far along are you?" they'd ask. To which I loved just to stare at them quizzically and say, "Huh? What do you mean?" Ah, the looks on their faces would be absolutely precious. But then if they hadn't run off, I'd answer.

"About seven months," I'd say and attempt to continue walking or shopping or peeing.

"Seven months?" they'd repeat incredulously.

"With twins," I'd say. The women's faces would inevitably go from admiring to worrying.

"You can't be having twins. You're way too small. Are you sure? You barely look pregnant." Luckily, most people who stop you on the street to comment on your pregnancy are licensed obstetricians, so they definitely know what they're talking about, which is comforting because otherwise a comment like that could make you feel *bad*.

"Nothing to worry about. I'm smoking a few packs a day to try to keep 'em slim," I'd say deadpan.

After a few encounters like that, I just stopped telling anyone I was having twins. It was too depressing.

Twenty-one days later, I was back in Uncle Remus's office, this time with Jon by my side to help fend off any wayward animated critters. I was feeling fairly hopeful that all the excess calories I'd been sucking down had gone straight to Sadie's hips, but, no, this was not the case. In fact, she'd only gained a couple of ounces and was still under two pounds. Baby A had gained a pound and I had put on roughly twenty pounds. If Uncle Remus tried to put a good spin on this, I swear I was ready to shoot the bluebird right off of his shoulder. Thankfully much less cheery, the doctor went to discuss his findings with my obstetrician over the phone while my husband and I sat and waited . . . and waited . . . and waited.

When he finally returned, the news wasn't good. "Sadie's placenta is too small, and she's not thriving in your uterus. It's not likely she'll grow any more, but we're going to try to keep you pregnant to buy Baby A more time in the womb." I was to go straight to the hospital to be given steroid shots to help the babies' lungs develop and to be monitored with the idea that I may have to deliver the babies in the next forty-eight hours. My head was spinning. But even if Sadie stayed stable, I would deliver the babies in two weeks. That's when it hit me that there was no way I would be taking my babies home with me when I left the hospital because in the best-case scenario, my twins would be six weeks premature.

My life was *so* not going as planned.

As usual, I kept my dignity intact for a solid three seconds and then sobbed like a twelve-year-old at a Jonas Brothers concert.

My new digs at the hospital weren't so bad. I wasn't in labor, which meant I wasn't in pain or on any kind of medication that can make you shake or feel muddled, so I spent my time trying to come up with a second baby moniker. I Googled baby names and emailed them to my husband, who emailed right back, "I am not naming my child Delancey. What about Katherine?" Clearly one of us was drinking and it wasn't me.

A couple of days into my stay, I developed a massive headache. I couldn't figure out what was going on, so after a few Tylenol and no relief, the nurse offered to get me a cup of coffee to see if a little caffeine would help. "Oh, thanks so much, but I already had a cup this morning with breakfast and I only want to drink one cup a day," I said, startling myself with my responsible attitude.

"Um, that's decaf they bring from the cafeteria, hon," the nurse said.

"Yeah, no, I *specifically* marked that I wanted regular coffee on my menu. They give you a choice of regular or decaf and I mark regular every day."

"I'm sure you do mark off the 'regular' box, but the cafeteria does not deliver caffeinated coffee to the pregnancy unit no matter what you ask for," the nurse said gently. *Were these people trying to kill me? I couldn't believe I fell right into their trap. What would be next? Would the morphine drip post-C-section be switched with Folgers to see if I noticed?* I would have to be on guard from now on. Caffeine-withdrawal headaches are a pretty nasty breed. "But I will sneak you some from the nurses' station," she added kindly. I instantly put her in my will.

The worst part of being in the hospital was not the boredom, the food, or even the coffee prohibition—it was being away from my almost three-year-old daughter, Elby. My heart ached for her all day every day. I'd never been away from her for more than one night at a time, and I'd never missed a day of taking her to preschool or picking her up in the short time since she'd started attending.

My husband would bring her to see me every day, and every day I'd get up, get dressed, and try to pretend everything was normal so that she wouldn't be frightened by all the monitors and wires. But each time she entered the door to my hospital room, she was scared. Sometimes she would give me a hug but then barely look at me. She asked her dad questions incessantly as if I wasn't there: "What's wrong with my mommy?" "Why isn't she coming home with us?" "Where are the Sun Chips?" My daughter became obsessed with Sun Chips, which either means she was hyperfocusing on something tangible to help her cope with the fear and confusion of a situation she didn't have the capacity to fully comprehend *or* she just really, *really* enjoyed the cheddary whole grainy goodness of a Sun Chip. Either way, totally understandable, but no matter, it broke my heart. I'd put on my bravest face when it was time for her to go and then I'd cry and start counting down the minutes until I could have my Ambien, the only recreational drug they give to pregnant ladies.

Amazingly, during the days and nights I endured mostly alone in my room, I spent very little time trying to imagine what it would be like to have a two-pound baby. I was worried—but my worry still didn't have a concrete base. It was like worrying about an alien invasion; it felt scary but distant, removed, shapeless. And I had no proof that Sadie was in fact two pounds; maybe she'd pop out and be five pounds—surprising the hell out of everyone. I'd heard ultrasound measurements could be off anyway. Maybe not by three pounds but, hey, if *The View*'s Sherri Shepherd could believe the earth is flat, I could believe my baby might be huge.

"This is Doctor Banks. He's one of the heads of our neonatal intensive care unit," a nurse announced to me one afternoon as she brought in a man dressed in a white coat over a pair of Dockers. He had oversize glasses and very sensitive eyes like a golden retriever, and I liked him immediately. I did want to get him fitted with some hipper frames, but I figured that could wait until after the babies were born.

"So, do you have any questions about our unit?" he asked, taking a seat in the one chair in the room and leaning forward. I had no idea what to ask. I'd never even seen the inside of a NICU.

"Um, well, if my baby only weighs two pounds, and that's a big *if*, because I've been eating dessert here with every meal, even the Jell-O. But if she does, how long do you think she'll have to be here?"

"I can't say for sure, but I'd expect them both to be here until their due date."

"Mmhmmm, that's a long time." Those sensitive eyes were not helping me keep it together. I stared at the television, which was showing a marathon of *Project Runway*, with the sound off. I noticed how the TV just hung there from the wall with just those small metal brackets to support it. It seemed so precarious. "And, um, a baby that's . . . um, really small . . ." I swallowed hard. "Is she going to be okay?"

"Yes. She's going to be fine. This is one of the best NICUs in the country. We're not a teaching hospital."

"Okay. Good." This was actually a huge relief because I had imagined an ugly scenario with clumsy *Grey's Anatomy* interns shoving each other out of the way in their overexcitement to learn the correct placement of an IV in a microscopic vein.

"Your babies will be in good hands. Not only that, but babies who are stressed in utero are better prepared for life outside of the womb. The stress hormones help their lungs develop faster." And then I got a tour of the NICU, where I got to see my first two-pound baby. And then it all became very real.

About ten days into my hospital stay, it was determined that because Sadie had remained stable, I would be allowed to go home for Thanksgiving, which was in two days, provided I came back the day afterward to be checked and then again on Monday, and if all was still okay I'd be scheduled for a C-section the following Thursday, right at my thirty-four-week mark. I was feeling upbeat. I packed my bags, watched one more episode of *Project Runway*, which I was now addicted to, and even passed on my evening Ambien. But then I thought better of it and took it anyway.

On Thanksgiving, my brother, Michael, my sister-in-law, Racquel, and my husband and I celebrated my homecoming by cooking a huge turkey with all the trimmings, making butternut squash soup from scratch and, naturally, my famous candied pecan pie. Okay, we ordered the entire meal precooked from the supermarket, but it was still incredible to eat food that didn't get delivered on a plastic tray with a warm diet soda by a surly hospital worker.

That night I read my daughter as many stories as she'd allow me to.

"Mommy, no more hos-pit-able, right? Are you all done?" Elby asked, in the middle of our third reading of *Froggy Takes a Bath*.

"Almost, baby. I have to go one more time but only for a couple of days when they take the babies out. Then I'll be home and I don't have to go anymore."

"Okay." Then five minutes later, "Mommy, no more hos-pit-able?"

The next day I went to be monitored. Everything was still fine.

Monday Jon took Elby to school while I went to be monitored one last time before my babies would be born on Thursday. And again, everything was fine. Next, I met Jon across the street at the high-risk office so Old Uncle Remus could get one last look-see. He started out as his usual annoyingly cheerful self, but then said nothing during my examination and abruptly left the room. "I'm having these babies today," I said.

"What do you mean?" Jon asked.

"He's not whistling. Something's wrong." Uncle Remus walked back into the exam room.

"Well, Sadie needs to come out, so you're having the babies today."

Lying on a bed in a hospital room with my C-section looming put a sense of urgency into naming Baby A. I mean, at this point I really didn't care what we named her, as long as it wasn't *any* of the suggestions my husband had made. Thumbing through a magazine, I spotted the name Matilda— cute, old-fashioned, and not reeking of Connecticut. I sprung it on Jon when he finally appeared minutes before I would be wheeled into surgery. He'd gone home to make arrangements for our daughter and to pack me a bag. "I kind of like that name—yeah, I really like it."

"Done," I called out as I was being wheeled off to get a spinal.

Now on the operating table in a fetal position on the verge of a panic attack, I tried to steady my breathing while the anesthesiologist attempted to find the exact spot between my vertebrae to insert the IV. He made small talk while he worked. "So what do you do?" he asked, poking a needle around my back.

"I'm a writer," I said, starting to shake. *Please, let my babies be okay,* I repeated over and over in my head like a mantra.

"You're kidding! Fantastic! What do you write?"

"Huh?"

"Have you written anything I've heard of?"

"I've written on a few crappy TV shows and I've written a couple of books about motherhood." *Please, let my babies be okay, God. I promise not to bitch endlessly about my pregnancy weight. Just let them cry when they come out.*

"That is such a coincidence. I'm a writer, too." *Was this guy kidding?*

"Well, I hope you have your anesthesiologist hat on today," I said just as I felt the sting of the needle find its place in the soft spot of my spine. My toes started feeling ever so slightly numb.

"I wrote a medical book on anesthesia for other doctors. It's a very different market, that's for sure. Who's your publishing company, if you don't mind my asking?" My legs were now useless. He had me right where he wanted me.

Nurses and doctors started to pack the tiny room like a balloon filling with air. There was a team of about six NICU doctors and nurses for each twin, plus my OB, her assistant surgeon, and about fourteen others moving around. Two of the NICU nurses on the team closest to me were having a conversation about their recent vacation to Palm Springs as if nothing out of the ordinary was going on. I had to try to keep reminding myself that I wasn't some huge medical mystery— I wasn't a guy with a record-setting forty-pound tumor or the recipient of the very first chimp to human kidney transplant. I was just a woman having babies a few weeks early. This was probably fairly routine to them. *But only the most foreign thing ever to happen to me.*

"No offense, but I'm about to have a two-pound baby and I'm scared shitless. Can't you push a little Valium through that IV?" I asked the anesthesiologist, ignoring his full-court networking.

"Sorry, can't do it. But I'll get you the good stuff as soon as the babies are out. So, Random House?"

"Simon Spotlight," I grunted. I certainly didn't want to lose my good drug privileges.

"How are they with publicity? My book hasn't done as well as I feel it could have. Textbooks are a toughie to promote." At this point I would've put a foot up his ass if I had any feeling in it whatsoever. Luckily, just then my husband was brought into the room, which, thankfully, ended our little book chat. I've never been so happy to see him in all my life. Jon had been as anxious as I was, especially since he suspected Sadie may not be much bigger than a six-inch sub.

A blue tent was draped over my body from my neck down.

"Here we go," came the disembodied voice of my OB. My husband gripped my hand, and I cried as I felt some pressure and then heard a mewing sound, like a newborn kitten. But it was Sadie and she was crying—all two pounds, six ounces of her—followed minutes later by a crying Matilda, who weighed in at a monstrous four pounds, four ounces. The most impossibly small babies were placed next to my face so that I could take in their new baby smell and see that they were all right, and then they were whisked off to the NICU while I was left to wait for feeling to return to my legs. It had finally returned to my heart.

"So, did you do any TV appearances for your book?" The ambitious gas passer popped back into my line of vision. Jon had gone with the babies, promising to return soon, and it was just the two of us left in the room. I gave up.

"Yeah."

"Oh, wow. Any suggestions on how I could get on TV to help get the word out there on my book?"

"Maybe you should try getting a job consulting on a medical show, then they could put your book on their website. Or find a private PR company that specializes in textbooks."

"Hey, thanks! That's a really good idea. Do you have any contacts?"

"That depends—do you have any better drugs?" My legs got enough feeling back to move me to recovery right in the nick of time.

* * *

These days, Sadie and Matilda are happy, healthy, running around, and, most important, sleeping through the night.

But it wasn't always this way. The babies developed severe colic when we got home from the NICU. At first I thought I would lose my mind between the constant screaming, postpartum depression, the worry, the endless doctor's visits, the mounting medical bills, and the crushing sleep deprivation. There were days—and especially nights—I didn't think I would make it through. I complained incessantly. I ranted and raved about how horrible and hard it was. Jon buried himself in work and the Internet, while simultaneously taking on night feedings so I could sleep, ordering us take-out food, and attending every doctor's appointment he could. One evening the babies were being particularly colicky, and Jon was calmly trying to look through the mail. In a fit of frustration, I yelled, "Why is this so easy for you and so hard for me? Are you made of stone? Don't you hear them screaming? I don't get it. I don't get *you*."

Jon said so simply and so sensibly, "I'm having a horrible time of it, too, trust me. But we deal with things differently. I figure the whole first year is going to suck. Just like the Pirate Ship."

He was exactly right. Just like the Pirate Ship, I needed to cry and scream and commiserate with anyone who was in the same boat, I needed to let Jon know that I wanted to get off, that we'd made a mistake. And just like the Pirate Ship, Jon stood right there by my side, knowing there was nowhere to go and intent on videotaping every moment until we made it to shore.

Acknowledgments

I am unbelievably lucky to be part of the whole SSE family but I would especially like to thank Patrick Price, my editor, for being my Sherpa, helping me shape this book with your expert eye, and most of all, knowing when to hold my hand and when to let it go. The big cheese, Jen Bergstrom, your sense of humor, effusiveness, loyalty, and friendship mean everything to me! Jennifer Robinson, your hard work, dedication, and endless supply of postage make my books possible. A huge debt of gratitude to Michael Nagin for the kick-ass cover.

Andy Barzvi, the easiest agent I've ever worked with and that's saying a lot! Thank you for your endless enthusiasm, wisdom, and for always taking my calls!

Thank you Brian Frazer, Chris Mancini, and Irene Zutell for reading chapters and giving invaluable feedback. And also

to Lisa Sundstedt, Cecily Knobler, Kelly and Miriam, and everyone in my circle of friends for your support.

Thanks to my kiz, Diana Horn, for constantly being my sounding board, my stylist, my bagel buddy, my photographer, and my platonic life partner!

Very special thanks to Heidi Lipka and Carolyn Lindsey. You knew how it was back then and how great it can be now!

Thank you to all my blogging pals for your support, laughs, comments, community, and encouragement. You kept me sane through everything that was going on while I was writing this book.

If I didn't have my brother Michael Wilder and sister-in-law Racquel, I would be residing in a loony bin somewhere far far away where I couldn't be a danger to other people. You've both gone way beyond the call of duty as family members—saving my life over and over—being my best friends and the greatest aunt and uncle my kids could ever wish for. And you've only gotten multiple orders of steamed dumplings in return. I owe you so big time.

I couldn't have written this book without my life preserver, the Jaguar, Lizbeth Gonzalez. Thank you for providing my twins the very next best thing to me while I was crying over having twins and then writing this book while *having twins*. You are joyful, loving, funny and I'm so grateful to have you in our lives. P.S. Wanna take it outside?

Elby, my ladybug, I love you more and more every minute. Seriously. It's crazy. I had no clue being a mom would be this cool. And yes, I want to see you dance. Daily.

Sadie and Matilda—my little sweet miracles: Your smiles make it all worthwhile. I appreciate you finally allowing me to sleep.

Jon—my deadlines are as hard on you as they are on me. Thank you for your patience, for letting me share things about our life, for being my rock, for making me laugh even when I'm crying, and for telling me what a Sherpa is. But mostly, thank you for making the last ten years the very happiest time in my life so far. I'm proud that you are my husband. In the immortal words of Bryan Adams, everything I do, I do it for you.

And lastly, to Oprah. Thank you in advance for most probably making my book your newest book club selection (I can't see why you wouldn't)! I've already told all my friends so let's make this happen!